D1105373

SAINTS
AND
STONES

SAINTS AND STONES

A GUIDE TO THE PILGRIM WAYS OF PEMBROKESHIRE

Damian Walford Davies
and
Anne Eastham

First Impression – 2002

ISBN 1 84323 124 7

© Damian Walford Davies and Anne Eastham
in association with the Saints and Stones Group.

Damian Walford Davies and Anne Eastham have asserted their right under the Copyright,
Designs and Patents Act, 1988, to be identified as Authors of this Work.

All rights reserved. No part of this book may be reproduced, stored in a retrieval
system, or transmitted in any form or by any means, electronic, electrostatic,
magnetic tape, mechanical, photocopying, recording or otherwise without
permission in writing from the publishers, Gomer Press, Llandysul, Ceredigion.

Printed in Wales at
Gomer Press, Llandysul, Ceredigion

In cities that
have outgrown their promise people
are becoming pilgrims
again, if not to this place,
then to the recreation of it
in their own spirits.

R.S. Thomas

CONTENTS

Preface

by the Right Reverend David Huw Jones,
retired Bishop of St Davids

It gives me great pleasure to commend this book describing the Saints and Stones pilgrimage trails in north Pembrokeshire. These trails have proved very popular with both local people and the many visitors who come to that lovely area on holiday. This is not surprising: they give visitors' journeys a sense of purpose and direction; they lead to ancient sites of great significance, located in beautiful surroundings; they enable those who are interested in history and architecture to delve back into the foundations of Christianity in west Wales; and those seeking spiritual refreshment will find places on these trails where prayers have been offered for centuries and where a sense of hallowed peace is virtually tangible. We thank those who have planned the trails and those who make the visits possible. Long may these pathways attract and delight visitors and encourage them to become pilgrims.

Foreword

by the Right Reverend Ivor Rees,
retired Bishop of St Davids

Saints and Stones! An imaginative title for an imaginative concept – the (re)creation of a pilgrimage trail linking ancient churches and emphasising the spiritual inheritance of north Pembrokeshire. This is very much the country of Dewi, Teilo and Brynach and of lesser-known saints who brought the Christian Faith to a pagan people and established the *llannau* around which communities would settle and grow.

We are indebted to those who had both the vision and the determination to initiate this enterprise, and to the Preseli-Pembrokeshire Council of the day, through Menter Preseli, for providing the support and the means to realise that vision. With the enthusiasm of clergy and parishioners, the first trail linked churches along the western seaboard, following one of the ancient pilgrimage routes to the shrine of St David in the Cathedral.

As one who had served in the area at various times in my ministry, I was – and still am – very conscious of the responsibility which is ours, so I was pleased and proud, as Bishop at that time, to be asked to be part of the launch of this enterprise in August 1995. The then Chairman of the Council – Councillor Lynn Davies – inaugurated the trail, while I was privileged to ask God's blessing on the venture and on all the pilgrims who would follow this ancient route. Although by then retired, I was also privileged to be present at the initiation of the two subsequent trails starting from Llanfyrnach in the north and from Llawhaden in the east of the county.

Sadly, although Menter Preseli continued to function, local government re-organisation in 1996 meant a shift in hands-on involvement and an end to the European funding which had aided the enterprise. Again, we are indebted to the dedicated band of clerics and lay people who, undaunted, continue to ensure that the trails are kept open, and continue to encourage pilgrims to follow them.

Our Cathedral Church of St Davids and the other churches described in this book remain an abiding testimony to the richness and variety of our heritage as well as to its antiquity. This is especially so when we recall that the sites are older than the buildings which still stand upon them, and that the worship of God and the prayers of the faithful continue to sanctify them after fifteen long centuries.

Worn by wind and weather, altered, enlarged, restored: these ancient *llannau* are often the only buildings that have survived in the flux of our national and social life, still used for their original purpose and still witnessing to the Faith in which they were founded. Saints and Stones is a venture that seeks to ensure that these ancient shrines and the trails which link them will give inspiration and deeper meaning to the lives of all who follow them.

'May the Lord bless your going out and your coming in from this time forth and for evermore.'

Glossary

Aumbry: A small recess for storage in the wall of a church.

Bailey: The defended outer ward of a medieval castle.

Bellcote: A masonry structure housing church bells. A feature of north Pembrokeshire churches.

Cantref: A Welsh territorial and administrative unit.

Chantry chapel: A privately endowed, often family, chapel in a church. Originally, the monks or priest would be charged with the duty of 'chanting' Masses for the soul of the founder.

Chapter house: Originally, the place where monks met to hear a chapter of the monastic rule; the meeting house of a cathedral.

Cist: A stone-lined grave.

Clas: A pre-Norman monastic community of the Welsh Church.

Corbel: A stone projecting from a wall to act as a support for a structure such as a rood-screen or second floor.

Easter Sepulchre: An elaborately decorated structure, initially of wood and later of stone, representing Christ's tomb, around which Easter celebrations were focused in pre-Reformation churches. The Host was kept in the sepulchre from Maunday Thursday until Easter morning.

Greek cross: A cross whose arms are all of equal length.

Host: The bread or wafer consecrated at the Eucharist, representing the body of Christ.

Latin cross: A cross whose lower vertical arm is longer than the horizontal.

Llan: Technically, the enclosure within which a church stands.

Maltese cross: A cross with splayed arms that are often curved or bifurcated at the ends.

Motte: A defensive mound of earth which would have been surmounted by a tower and wooden fence.

Ogham (or Ogam): A writing system, developed in Ireland before the 5th century AD, comprising twenty characters inscribed as groups of notches or strokes along the edge of a stone.

Piscina: A stone basin in the chancel of pre-Reformation churches used to wash communion vessels.

Rath: An Iron Age enclosure surrounded by strong earth banks.

Reliquary: A small receptacle in which the relics of a saint are kept.

Rood-screen and rood-loft: An elaborately carved wooden screen, surmounted by a crucifix, dividing the nave from the chancel in pre-Reformation churches. A loft or gallery ran across the top of the screen. Comparatively few survive.

Sanctus bell: A bell situated at the junction of the nave and chancel. It was rung to summon the congregation to church and also tolled during the Sanctus hymn.

Squinch: As encountered in some Pembrokeshire churches, a small arched or vaulted space in a church, perhaps enclosing the original cell of the founding saint.

Squint: Also known as a hagioscope or leper's squint – a passage or opening cut in the chancel (or other) wall to allow the congregation in an aisle or side-chapel (or those outside the church) to see the elevation of the Host at the High Altar.

Tracery: Ornamented stonework in the upper part of a window.

Water stoup: A small vessel attached to the wall of a church, usually near the entrance, containing holy water.

Weeping chancel: A chancel that lies at a pronounced angle to the nave (the 'weep' is usually to the north); traditionally so called since such a configuration recalls the bowed head of the crucified Christ.

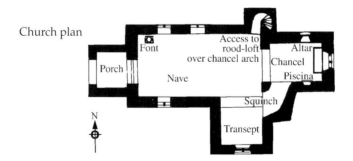

Church plan

Time line

Approximate Dates	Period
3,500 BC	Early Neolithic or New Stone Age
2,500 BC	Late Neolithic
2,000 BC	Early Bronze age
1,300 BC	Late Bronze Age
600 BC	Iron Age
AD 43	Roman Period
AD 400	Early Medieval Period or Dark Ages
AD 1066	Medieval Period
AD 1485	Early Modern Period

Introduction

Thus says the Lord: Stand at the crossroads and look and ask for the ancient paths where the good way lies; and walk in it and find rest for your souls.

Jeremiah 6, 16

It is nearly 1,500 years since the first Christian pilgrims travelled the western sea routes which led from Mediterranean Europe through Brittany and Cornwall to Pembrokeshire and Ireland. Many of these early saints – usually scions of the princely families of Brittany, Ireland and Wales – had journeyed far and wide, to Rome or Jerusalem for example, in their search for spiritual fulfilment before settling in north Pembrokeshire to establish religious houses and mission stations within the context of the social structure of west Wales in the 6th century.

Men like St David, St Brynach, St Justinian, St Teilo, St Colman, St Hywel and St Gwyndaf and even St Patrick for a brief period, established themselves in Pembrokeshire. They founded their communities as 'clas' churches, gathering around themselves disciples and converts to the Christian church. These converts proclaimed their new allegiance in memorial stones dating from the 5th to the 10th century which are found throughout north Pembrokeshire. Even in their own day, these missionary saints were revered and admired for their devotion and energetic promulgation of Christianity. From infancy, they were credited with miraculous powers and the story of their lives became an integral part of the religious heritage of the early church in the west. Their saintly exploits were recorded during the 11th and subsequent centuries with an immediacy which emphasises how fresh and relevant these figures were to contemporary society.

There is architectural and archaeological evidence that many of the churches dedicated to these 6th-century saints were built prior to the Cymro-Norman settlement of Pembrokeshire. They are small, sunk into the land of which they are a part, breathtakingly simple, and preserve an atmosphere of peace and contemplation. Many are surrounded by circular enclosures which may belong to a prehistoric settlement in the region. Over the centuries, these churches have at various times fallen into decay and have been rebuilt and modified, reflecting changing economic and social conditions.

The Saints and Stones trails have been set up to give both holiday visitors and residents in the county access to some of the more remote and beautiful corners of Pembrokeshire and to the deep spiritual quality of these ancient places of worship. In July 1995, the first trail was launched by Bishop Ivor Rees with the backing of Menter Preseli and the EU leader programme II. A trail leaflet and individual leaflets for each church were scripted and designed by members of the Saints and Stones Group and printed and financed by Menter Preseli. In 1996, the project received a 'Commended' in the Schroder Tourism awards. At Eastertide 1998, the 'In the Shadow of the Preselis' trail was launched, led by Bishop Huw Jones. During Lent 1999, supported by both Bishop Huw and Bishop Ivor, a third route, 'The Bishop's Road', from the Bishop's Palace at Llawhaden to St Davids was opened. The trail leaflet for this project was entirely financed by donations from local people and businesses.

All three trails focus ultimately on St Davids, the Cathedral and the shrine of the saint. For the purposes of this book, we have divided the first half of the first trail, 'Pilgrims from the Sea', into two routes, one following the coast and one cutting inland; these routes converge on the way south towards St Davids. The tour 'In the Shadow of the Preselis' can be undertaken both as an independent trail and as the first half of a route that links up with the 'Pilgrims from the Sea' trail. 'The Bishop's Road' proceeds west, following the route known to medieval pilgrims as the Portway. There are a number of significant sites in the immediate vicinity of St Davids, and we have therefore included a fourth 'circuit' – 'Cylch Dewi – The Sacred Landscape of St David' – which centres on the area around the city.

Clear directions are given for each stage of the tour, but we recommend that the pilgrim also follow a good map. Ordnance Survey map references have been provided for all the sites to be visited on these trails. The OS sheets covering the pilgrim routes are in the Landranger (1:50,000 scale) and Explorer/Outdoor Leisure (1:25,000 scale) series: Landranger 145 – Cardigan and Surrounding Area; Landranger 157 – St Davids and Haverfordwest; Landranger 158 – Tenby/Dinbych-y-Pysgod; Explorer/Outdoor Leisure 35 – North Pembrokeshire; and Explorer/Outdoor Leisure 36 – South Pembrokeshire.

The Saints and Stones Group organises a diverse programme of religious and community events throughout the year. For the main annual pilgrimage in August, pilgrims from all over Britain and abroad gather at different churches along the three trails for worship and meditation and travel the lanes and byways by car or on foot to meet up for a communal lunch. In the afternoon there are guided visits to other churches along the way and finally a special welcome in the Cathedral. It is particularly uplifting to arrive in the company of 30 or 40 fellow pilgrims after hours on the road or across country, often in drenching rain, and participate in the simple words of a traditional evensong.

The churches are always open to pilgrims and visitors during daylight hours. The theme is a ministry of welcome. There is a dog bowl, a kettle, tea, coffee, squash and sometimes biscuits laid out for refreshment. The churches are not 'manned', but visitors are invited to sign the visitors' books. There is public access to every ancient monument mentioned, unless otherwise indicated. Where a monument is on private land, visitors should seek formal permission to view it. It is also vital that visitors should at all times observe the Country Code, keeping to designated footpaths and taking special care to fasten gates.

*   *   *

We would like to thank the Right Reverend Bishop Hugh Jones and the Right Reverend Bishop Ivor Rees for providing a Preface and Foreword to this book, and the Very Reverend John Wyn Evans, Dean of St Davids, for his support for the project. We are also grateful to members of the Saints and Stones Group for providing supplementary information, to Grizel Care for her line drawings, to Mike Eastham for the church plan, drawings and trail maps, and to the Reverend John Bennett of Llanrhian, Dr Nancy Edwards of the University of Wales, Bangor and Essie Beynon of Rhyd-y-Gath for their advice and assistance. Except where otherwise stated, all the photographs were produced by the authors or members of the Saints and Stones Group.

PILGRIMS FROM THE SEA

It was the highways of the sea that first brought many of the prehistoric peoples to west Wales. Along these routes came Neolithic farmers, the builders of megalithic tombs and the land-hungry peoples and traders of the Bronze and Iron Ages. They travelled up the Atlantic coasts of Spain and France to reach Brittany, across the land-bridge of that peninsula and on to Cornwall, Wales, north-west Britain and Ireland. Along the Pembrokeshire coast, there were major ports like Newport and Fishguard and many others like Dinas and Goodwick at which were landed fish, freight and people into the 17th century, as the Pembrokeshire surveyor and antiquarian George Owen recorded in his *Description of Penbrokshire* in 1603. From the points at which they arrived, they penetrated up the river valleys, establishing cultural groups and markets for their goods and ideas. We can trace the history of their movements in Pembrokeshire by the material remains still visible in the landscape and, to some extent, from living traditions and linguistic marks preserved in place names.

Many of these arrivals date from the 5th and 6th centuries AD, the Age of the Saints. These holy men came as pilgrims and missionaries to the shores of Pembrokeshire along the same routes as their prehistoric forbears, to land at the same harbours and to follow the same tracks across the countryside. These tracks are often marked by burial mounds or standing stones which acted in pairs as guide points indicating the safest route to follow, especially when crossing

The Lady Stone

boggy or difficult ground. One such is the **Lady Stone** (OS SM 996 376) in the hedge on the north side of the A487 road from Dinas to Fishguard. It is clear that many of these stones, though prehistoric in origin, were used by later travellers who in a sense re-dedicated them. A stone at Capel Colman near Boncath marks the prehistoric track over Frenni Fawr mountain; in early Christian times a 'rosace' pattern was inscribed on one face and a triangular-headed Latin cross with crossed arms on the other. This practice became even more extensive in medieval Brittany, where entire calvaries were carved onto prehistoric standing stones.

The Pilgrims from the Sea trail now divides in two, to meet up ultimately at Mathry. The first route continues through Fishguard to Llanwnda church, while the second (beginning on p. 18) cuts inland towards Llanllawer Holy Well. A cross stone in a nearby field called Parc Maen Dewi bears the marks of early Christian pilgrims.

Pilgrims from the Sea

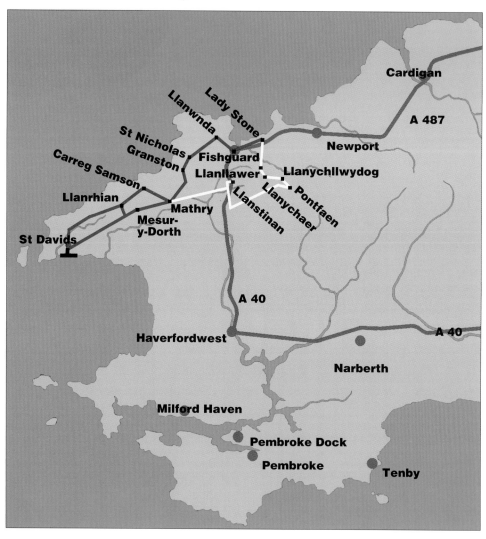

Cardigan

A 487

Llanwnda

Lady Stone

Newport

St Nicholas
Granston

Fishguard

Llanllawer

Llanychllwydog

Carreg Samson

Llanstinan

Llanychaer

Pontfaen

Llanrhian

Mathry

Mesur-
y-Dorth

St Davids

A 40

Haverfordwest

A 40

Narberth

Milford Haven

Pembroke Dock

Pembroke

Tenby

— Route A

Route B

— Mathry – St Davids

Route A

Llanwnda Church (St Gwyndaf) OS SM 932 396

From Fishguard, proceed to Goodwick and take the steep road signposted to Llanwnda (take care at the hairpin bend at the crest of the hill). After 0.3ml, take the right fork, and after another 0.3ml, turn left and proceed down into the village.

Pilgrims on their way to Llanwnda, having climbed the steep slope of Penrhiw, would have been directed down to the village by an ancient

Penrhiw
Waymarker

waymarker inscribed at a later date with a double-outline Latin cross which is still situated in the hedgebank on the right as one takes the final left turn down to the village. Standing in an exposed, wind-swept position among farmsteads on Pen Caer peninsula overlooking the Atlantic, St Gwyndaf's church, dating back beyond the 8th century, is an excellent example of the rugged simplicity so characteristic of north Pembrokeshire churches. It is also a palpable

reminder of the early saints' liking for the isolated and elemental. The great medieval scholar and cleric, Giraldus Cambrensis – Gerald of Wales or Gerald de Barri (*c.*1146–1223) – held the living at Llanwnda for a while. The double-bellcote church (the second bellcote used to house the Sanctus bell)

St Gwyndaf's, Llanwnda

St Gwyndaf badge
(Goodwick C.P. School)

St Gwyndaf (6th century)

Feast Day: 6 November

Gwyndaf Hen ('The Aged'), a Breton, was the son of Emyr Llydaw and brother of Amwn Ddu. He married Gwenonwy, a daughter of Meurig ap Tewdrig, and their son became St Meugan. He was a confessor at the great college of Llanilltud Fawr and a chaplain in the monastery of St Dyfrig (Dubricius) at Caerleon. He is also considered to be the founder of Llanwnda in Caernarfonshire and to have retired to Bardsey Island off the Llŷn peninsula – the burial-place of 20,000 saints – where he died.

Known as a rather irascible character, Gwyndaf was returning to Llanwnda from Fishguard over a boundary stream after a contretemps with the Irishman St Aidan when a fish leapt suddenly, causing Gwyndaf's horse to rear up and its rider to fall and break his leg. The injured saint promptly cursed the stream so that it remained fishless ever after. This temper sometimes got him into difficulties. Another story tells how Gwyndaf and Aidan, on their way to St Davids, paused at Tregroes Well in the parish of Whitchurch. Each was anxious to give his name to the holy well, and an unseemly, unsaintly brawl was the result. Gwyndaf was soundly beaten, and a smug Aidan promptly dedicated the well to himself and went on his way west. A bruised Gwyndaf slouched north to Llanwnda, where he had the pleasure of founding a church and consecrating his own well – Ffynnon Wnda – nearby.

was heavily but sympathetically restored in 1881, preserving its medieval character. The two modern bells at the west end are dedicated to St David and St Patrick in memory of the crews of two cross-channel steamers sunk in the Second World War.

The church has many features of great historic interest. In the porch is a 'leper's squint', through which the unfortunate sufferers could view the elevation of the Host at the High Altar. Prior to the restoration of 1881, the church had been derelict for some years; the stone (Norman) font had been placed for safekeeping in a nearby cottage. The church once had a rood-loft; today, only the supporting corbels protruding from the wall remain. On one of the 15th-century roof-beams, the face of a tonsured monk has been carved in high relief. Note also the vaulted ceiling. Two piscinae were discovered during restoration work: one, a plain, circular bowl, is in the south wall of the chancel while the other is in the south transept (originally a chantry chapel). On the

Llanwnda roof-beam

window-sill near the font is a fragment of a medieval stone showing a bishop administering a blessing and holding a staff; it may have been part of an ancient churchyard cross. Another stone fragment of the same date can be seen on the first window-sill in the south wall. In the chancel is a case containing a copy of the Welsh 'Parry' Bible (1620).

Carved face, Llanwnda

No fewer than six 7th–9th-century Christian marked stones were also discovered in 1881; five of them are set into the exterior walls of the church. Once part of larger structures, they were carved by stonemasons working under monastic patronage. The most fascinating of these is set into the east end of the south transept. It shows a rudely incised face surrounded by four parallel lines beneath the cross of St Andrew; the face may be that of a female, a monk or Christ-as-Pantocrator. High in the south wall is a stone marked with a double-

7

outline cross and another in the east wall of the chancel is decorated with a Latin cross. A fourth stone in the north wall displays a double Latin cross enclosed by a rounded outline, and low in the south wall to the west of the porch is a stone of later date (probably 10th century) with a moulded cross. The base of a decorated cross lies on the north-west side of the churchyard.

Beyond a wooden gate, a short distance to the south of the churchyard, is Ffynnon Wnda, a holy well. Llanwnwr farm and manor, on the west side of Pen Caer near Strumble Head, is thought to be the site of a sister-church of St Gwyndaf's: graves have been found in the farmyard.

Ffynnon Wnda

Though insulated now from all the noise and commotion of modern life, the area around Llanwnda was once the scene of violence and the focus of a nation's anxieties. A memorial stone on the coast at Carregwastad Point, a little over 0.5ml along a footpath north-west of the church, marks the spot where the last invasion of mainland Britain – by a motley force of 1,400 French soldiers – took place on 22 February 1797. The French were under the command of an American veteran, Colonal William Tate, and Trehowel farm near Llanwnda was commandeered as their headquarters. The belief that Llanwnda church was sacked and burned during the invasion, which collapsed after two days, surely exaggerates a more mundane truth. The cold, wet and tired French soldiers, having struggled up the cliffs, and unloaded firearms, probably lit a small fire in the church to keep warm during those cold February days. The parish register for 1797 has pages missing: they were probably used by the French as kindling. The chalice and church plate were plundered by the invaders but subsequently recovered in a pawn shop in Carmarthen and returned to Llanwnda. Some 2ml west of Carregwastad Point is Pen Capel Degan, reputed to be the site of a medieval chapel.

Garn Wnda burial chamber

The presence of many megalithic remains in the vicinity points to the fact that Pen Caer was a place of great importance in the Neolithic period and Bronze Age. On Garn Wnda – the bracken-covered, boulder-strewn hillside behind the church – is an impressive 4th–early 3rd millennium BC burial chamber (OS SM 933 392). Its huge capstone is supported on the downhill side by a sidestone while the other side rests on the ground – a type of cromlech known as an 'earth-fast' tomb. The chamber was excavated in the late 19th century; archaeologists discovered an urn containing cremated bones. Other burial chambers are located 1.5ml west at Garn Gilfach and 0.5ml and 1ml east in Harbour Village, Goodwick.

St Nicholas Church (St Nicholas)

From Llanwnda, return to the third junction and turn right. Two routes to St Nicholas are possible. One can continue on this road around the peninsula, initially following signs for Strumble Head, skirting the spectacular Iron Age hillforts of Garn Fawr and Garn Fechan and then down into St Nicholas at Trefasser Cross; alternatively, the pilgrim may take the route that cuts inland after 0.3ml, signposted to St Nicholas, turning right into the village at the junction after 3ml.

Known as Tremarchog ('The Knight's Estate') in Welsh and 'Villa Camerarii' ('The Chamberlain's Estate' – a reference to an official of episcopal lands) in Latin documents, St Nicholas is a peaceful, picturesque village not far from the beautiful coves of Aber Bach and Pwll Deri. The village takes its English name from the church dedication to the patron saint of children and sailors. With its single bellcote, the church last saw major restoration work in 1865. Its origins are uncertain: it has been suggested that a Christian foundation was established here by the end of the Roman period. Inside, kneelers depicting local buildings, scenes and landscapes add colour to the restful simplicity of the nave. In the south transept is an interesting architectural feature known as a 'squinch', characteristic of many Pembrokeshire churches such as Llanstinan: this vaulted space is thought to enclose the original cell of the founder hermit or saint. The font is Norman.

St Nicholas church

10

In the chancel are three 5th–6th-century Christian inscribed stones. As the historian Richard Fenton recorded in 1810, the large, rectangular stone now set into the base of the south chancel arch was once used as 'a stile in the wall of the churchyard to the east of the porch'; by 1873 it had been set into the

St Nicholas church, interior

churchyard wall and in 1905 it was brought into the chancel. At some unknown date, its surface suffered the indignity of being covered with a black substance, presumably in an attempt to make the inscription more visible. The Latin script reads 'TUNCCETACE UXSOR DAARI HIC IACIT' – 'Tunccetace, wife of Daarus, lies here.' In 1873, the Celtic scholar Sir John Rhŷs suggested that 'Tunccetace' would be rendered 'Tynghedog' – '[favoured by] fortune/fate' – in Welsh, reminiscent of such Latin names as 'Fortunatus' and 'Fortunata'. A primitive linear cross, probably 7th–9th century, has been cut into the lower right-hand side of the stone.

Tunccetace stone

Two other stones are set into the base of the north chancel arch. They were once used as gateposts on Llandruidion farm, 1.5ml north of the church – possibly the site of an early

11

St Nicholas badge
(Mathry V.C. School)

St Nicholas (5th century)

Feast Day: 6 December

St Nicholas was born in Patara in the province of Lycia in Asia Minor. From birth, he was precociously pious, able to pray for hours and fast, refusing milk on two days each week. In 425, he became Bishop of Myra in the same province and the story of his ministry contains accounts of the many miracles he performed to alleviate pain and poverty among his people. He saved a child from a raging fire and helped a poor man who could not provide dowries for his three daughters. All three were about to be cast out on the street with no prospect of marriage. Secretly, the saint crept out in the dark and, night by night, threw bags of money into the house so that each girl in turn was able to marry the man of her choice. During his passage to the Holy Land, he saved both ship and crew in a storm, thereby becoming the patron saint of sailors. He gained pardon for three men imprisoned in a tower – a story which developed and merged with the colourful tale of his resuscitation of three little boys who had been dismembered and placed in a pickling jar when the innkeeper ran out of bacon. Through this miracle he became a patron saint of children. In 1087, long after his death, his body was removed from Myra to Bari in southern Italy. A popular saint in medieval Britain, St Nicholas has five Pembrokeshire churches and chapels dedicated to him.

Christian settlement. One of the stones is inscribed with a small linear Latin cross and the name 'PAANI' – '[the stone of] Paanus'. Sir John Rhŷs conjectured that this is the memorial stone of one of the sons of the 5th-century Welsh king of Irish descent, Brychan Brycheiniog. Edward Lhuyd (1660–1709), the great botanist, linguist, antiquarian and Keeper of the Ashmolean Museum at Oxford, visited Llandruidion farm around 1690 to sketch this stone. It was clearly split at some point, presumably by the practical Pembrokeshire farmer who wished to reduce the size of the gatepost, since the stone as Lhuyd saw it was larger and carried another inscription. The

Dedication of village well, St Nicholas   (*photo:* Martin Cavaney)

second pillar-stone in the chancel bears the scars of its gatepost
existence in the shape of clearly visible holes – six on the face and
three on the left side – one of which has unfortunately rendered a
definitive reading of the inscription difficult. V. E. Nash-Williams in
1950 read the inscription as 'MELI' –'[the stone of] Melus' – with the
letters inverted and reversed.

A natural spring is located a short distance from the church; it
provided the village with water from medieval times until the 1940s
and is still used during water shortages. It was re-dedicated by
Bishop Hugh Jones during a pilgrimage in August 1995. Tradition
has it that the hamlet of Trefasser, 1.5ml north of St Nicholas, is the

birthplace of Asser, known as Asserius Menevensis (d. 909), counsellor to and biographer of King Alfred the Great of Wessex (though the place could quite easily be named after one of the numerous other Assers who figure in the ecclesiastical history of Pembrokeshire).

Three ancient features of the landscape in the vicinity of St Nicholas deserve a visit. One is the impressive standing stone, dating from the 2nd millennium BC, at Rhos y Clegyrn ('Moor of the Stones'), 0.75ml east of St Nicholas (OS SM 913 354), along a signed footpath off the inland road towards Llanwnda. The stone stands 2.7m high among gorse. Excavations during the 1960s revealed the installation-pit of a second stone, now lost, to the north-east. A cobbled pavement was discovered to have been laid discontinuously around and to the east of the paired stones. Under the cobbles in a layer of grey silt, fragments of cremated bone and pottery were found, and below them, the remains of seven sub-rectangular and elliptical huts. Their construction, and finds associated with them, suggest seasonal occupation at some point between the late Neolithic and late Bronze Age.

0.5ml south of St Nicholas is a Neolithic burial chamber known as the Trellys chamber or Ffyst Samson (St Samson's Flail) (OS SM 906 349). A walk from Trellys-draw farm leads through the gate up the hillside footpath opposite for 0.5ml to the moorland beyond. The tomb stands among gorse on a rocky plateau commanding stupendous vistas over the surrounding countryside towards St Davids Head and the sea. The enormous, rugged capstone rests delicately on two metre-high sidestones. It is a place where a sense of great age is palpable.

Medieval pilgrims travelling southwards to St Davids would

therefore have passed through a landscape bearing dramatic testimony to the religious beliefs and practices of ancient pagan civilisations.

From St Nicholas, motorists may decide to return to the A487 before taking the next turning right towards Granston. But it is possible to continue past the church along the narrow lane which leads to the old farm at Tresisillt, where a sharp left turn leads steeply down into the tangle of woods behind Aber Bach beach. A left turn at the bottom leads to the woollen mill and shop at Tregwynt, which is open to visitors all the year round.

Mills have been recorded in this valley at least since the Middle Ages, and in the bank on the west side of the lane down to Aber Bach it is still possible to see several levels of mill leat leading out of the stream to provide power for installations which used to exist on the descent to the beach. Climbing once more out of the valley, the road passes Tregwynt mansion. This was the home of the Harries family for many generations. In 1999 a coin hoard, buried in 1648 during the Civil War, was discovered there. It was hidden during the lifetime of Llewellyn Harries, who was known to have loyalist sympathies. A hundred and fifty years later, on the night of 22 February 1797, a ball was in progress and Colonel Thomas Knox, Commander of the Fishguard Fencibles, was in attendance. News of the arrival of a French invasion force at Carregwastad Point broke up the party, and the hostess and her sons left hastily in carriages with the rest.

St Catherine's, Granston

Less than 0.5ml inland from Tregwynt, Granston church stands on a mound beside the road. It looks out towards the hillfort of Garn Fawr on Pen Caer with ruffled glimpses of the sea between. The present building dates from 1877; it replaced the early medieval *Ecclesia Villa Grandi* which served the large episcopal manor nearby. The original foundations of the church seem to have been retained: Granston is a plain edifice of a nave and chancel with a squinch arch – lit from the outside by a small circular window – leading through what is now the north transept. The Victorian structure has retained much of the unadorned simplicity that appears to have characterised the earlier, medieval building. There are, however, some attractive modern embroideries on the theme of the loaves and fishes for the altar, lectern and pulpit hangings. The font is octagonal, sloping off to a circular shaft and base, probably of 14th-century date.

Squinch arch, Granston

St Catherine's Wheel – medieval pilgrim badge

St Catherine (3rd–4th century)

Feast Day: 25 November

There are numerous St Catherines in Christian hagiography. Granston church is most probably dedicated to St Catherine of Alexandria, who protested to Maxentius, the Roman Emperor (c. 306–12) about the worship of idols. Having refused to deny her Christian faith or marry the emperor, she was beaten and cast into prison, where, fed by a dove, she saw Christ in a vision. She survived an attempt to break her body on a spiked wheel – the Catherine wheel – and her constancy converted 200 soldiers to the faith. When she was finally beheaded, her arteries bled milk and her body was carried by angels to Mount Sinai, where a monastery was dedicated to her. Her cult was popular with pilgrims and isolated communities.

The *Taxatio* of 1291 and the *Black Book of St Davids* – an inventory of diocesan assets prepared for Bishop Martyn in 1326 – record that the benefice of Granston had connections with the Tironian monastery at St Dogmael's near Cardigan. When the parish was united with that of St Nicholas in 1534 during Rees Owen's tenure as vicar, the patronage of St Nicholas remained with the Bishop of St Davids, while that of Granston was attached to the Crown after the Dissolution.

Granston was the site of an episcopal court which collected rents and was responsible for ensuring that the tenants of the bishop performed their feudal duties at the appropriate season. To the north-west of the churchyard, a small stone enclosure containing a quantity of fallen stone rubble may, according to local tradition, be part of an early court building. The Welsh name for the manor – Treopert – points to the tenure of one Robert at an early stage in its history. Tradition associates Granston with Robert, one of the sons of William the Conqueror, but given the connection with St Dogmael's Abbey, it is possible that the Robert in question may be Robert FitzMartin of Cemais.

Route B

A short distance past the Lady Stone on the Dinas to Fishguard road, the alternative Pilgrims from the Sea route to Mathry, where both routes unite (p. 32), bears left off the A487 onto a minor road towards the village of Llanychaer.

Located in a field near the disused church of St David, at the point at which the lane begins to descend sharply towards the village, is **Llanllawer Holy Well** (OS SM 987 360). The church was rebuilt in the 19th century, incorporating two 9th- or 10th-century cross stones, one in the south wall, the other as a lintel on the north side. On the gateposts into the churchyard are carved two wheel-crosses. The churchyard itself was originally elliptical in shape. It is thought that many of the circular graveyards found in north Pembrokeshire and elsewhere are of ancient, in some cases pre-Christian, origin.

The well is a medieval voussoired vault over a clear bubbling spring. It has the remains of step or bench structures in the interior to assist in bodily immersion. Richard Fenton (1810) records it as a healing well, especially efficacious in the treatment of eye complaints, and it was by local tradition both a wishing and a cursing well. Coins and pins were offered, with a straight pin conferring a blessing and a bent pin misfortune on the object of the wish.

Llanllawer Holy Well

Looking south from this point, the view across the Gwaun valley into the Trecŵn gorge can be breathtaking. Out of the gorge flow the Aer and Nant y Bugail rivers, the one into the Gwaun, the other towards the Cleddau.

Opposite the well, a turning to the left leads up Mynydd Dinas. Just over 0.5ml from the turning, a line of four large stones stand towering above the road in the bank of a field called **Parc y Meirw** (OS SM 998 359). These are part of an alignment, other elements of which may still be seen along the banks on either side of the lane. These traces suggest that Parc y Meirw was once a megalithic avenue rather than a single alignment, and there is some evidence that it extended at one time as far as Trellwyn farm. The stones are aligned north-west; a bearing on them extends to the deep water channel to the north of the Tusker rock at the entrance to Wexford harbour in Ireland. This could be coincidence, but it is possible that the alignment was used as a navigation aid by its prehistoric builders.

The field name Parc y Meirw – 'field of the dead' – may derive from the battle of Mynydd Carn which is believed to have taken place nearby in 1081 and which is recorded in a contemporary poem by Meilyr Brydydd. During the course of the fighting, three Welsh princes – Trahaearn ap Caradog, Caradog ap Gruffudd and Meilyr ap Rhiwallon – were killed by the forces of Rhys ap Tewdwr of Deheubarth and Gruffudd ap Cynan, assisted by the Irish. Later that year, William the Conqueror came on expedition or pilgrimage to St Davids, secure in the knowledge that this encounter, which had eliminated so many of the Welsh leaders who might have opposed him, had significantly expedited his Cymro-Norman settlement of south Wales.

LLANYCHAER CHURCH (ST DAVID)   OS SM 992 345

Returning to Llanllawer Well, the road descends steeply into the village of Llanychaer, past Cwrt, a farm, which was upgraded to a gentry mansion around 1800, but which is now much decayed. At the T-junction of the B4313 from Fishguard to Maenclochog, it is possible to see the outline of a defended Iron Age enclosure behind the pub opposite. Bear left at the junction, and continue over the crossroads after 0.3ml. St David's church is located in a glade on the right.

There is a strange subaqueous greenness about Llanychaer churchyard, even in the depths of winter. The exact meaning of

St David's, Llanychaer

'Llanychaer' has not been definitively explained; early forms suggest it may signify 'the glade of the bondman/serf' or perhaps 'the glade of Aer', though nothing is known of this individual. The simple bellcote church was rebuilt in 1871. Inside, it is sparse and intimate, with the bare stone walls giving a sense of solidity. In the churchyard, amongst the tombs within railings, is an unusual 7th–9th-century Christian stone. On the north face, the crucified, bearded Christ is depicted in a tunic; note the pained expression and the ghostly, outstretched fingers. Below is a six-petalled flower within a circular

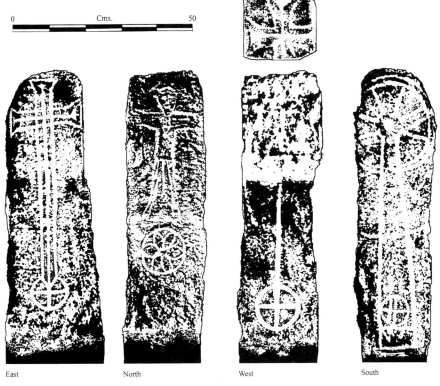

East   North   West   South

Crucifixion stone, Llanychaer

outline – an unusual motif for an inscribed stone in Pembrokeshire, though a number of similar decorations survive in Galicia, Spain. On the south face is an outline Latin ring-cross with splayed arms with a ring-cross at its base. Two further Latin crosses standing on ring-crosses are incised on the west and east faces (the former is badly damaged) while an outline Greek cross with fluted arms appears on the top of the stone. The visibility of the images is greatly improved during the summer months when the damp stone dries and the patterns emerge through the lichen that encrusts the stone.

21

From St David's church, return to the crossroads and bear right, following the signs for Cwm Gwaun.

A short distance from the crossroads, the pilgrim passes Y Garn on the right, a medieval hall house with later additions of a Flemish chimney and a slate roof which replaced the original thatch. The whole property has recently been modernised. The present bridge across the Gwaun at Cilrhedyn probably belongs to the time of the toll road but there are signs in the river banks that a much earlier bridge existed underneath the current structure. The route continues for 0.4ml alongside the river under the oak woods that cover the steep banks of what was once a glaciated U-shaped valley. Under the trees, the lances of the hart's tongue fern light the dark undergrowth with acid green. In spring, these woods are sprinkled with wood anemones, and the surrounding blackthorn bushes become white with blossom and blue with the lichens entwined around their twigs.

Pilgrim Way,
Gwaun valley

The present church at Llanychllwydog replaced an earlier building. A drawing of 1859 shows an interior similar to that of Pontfaen church at the time. Although the church today is a private house, access is permitted to the graveyard, in which stand four stones, each inscribed with a cross of a different design and finish. Two are on neatly dressed, squared bluestone blocks with well-cut Latin crosses in double or treble outline, one with a centre boss; a third bears a wheel-centered cross with each arm crossed; and the fourth – a much cruder block of rhyolite – is decorated with a simple, roughly chiselled cross. Richard Fenton believed that two of these stones marked the grave of Clydawc, the legendary founder of this church, but stylistic evidence suggests that they can probably be dated to somewhere between the 7th and 9th centuries AD.

Llanychllwydog church, interior (1859)

Latin cross,
Llanychllwydog churchyard

From Llanychllwydog, follow the Gwaun river upstream for 0.9ml to the village of Pontfaen, passing Tŷ Gwyn – now the Post Office but once the old toll gate on the road between Fishguard and Narberth. At Pontfaen, the road up to the church turns sharply right and climbs out of the Gwaun valley. Pontfaen ('the stone bridge') was an important crossing on a prehistoric route, now known as Ffordd Bedd Morris, from Newport to St Davids over Mynydd Caregog.

St Brynach hoped to settle here, having left Llanfyrnach and Henry's Moat. It is believed that he built the first church on the site in AD 540, but he failed to exorcise the devils who plagued him during the night and could not rest here.

The church is built within a circular rampart and ditch, very similar to the many promontory forts which guard the banks of the Gwaun. In the Middle Ages, Pontfaen was attached to Pill Priory, Milford Haven, which was a dependent priory of St Dogmael's Abbey. At the dissolution of the monasteries, ownership passed to the Prince of Wales. At that time, the church was similar in size and shape to the present structure, comprising a nave, chancel and a small chapel on the north side with a squinch which affords a view of the altar. There is some discussion as to the precise status of a

St Brynach's, Pontfaen

St Brynach badge
(Llanychllwyddog
C.P. School)

St Brynach (6th century)

Feast Day: 7 April

As one early account states, Brynach was an Irishman of noble birth, but 'Deeming not the land of his birth as his own', he resolved to 'acquire a country by pilgrimage' and 'went on his journey'. He travelled to Rome where he slew a monster, and returning to Wales via Brittany, accomplished the sea-crossing on his 'llech' or stone altar. At Milford, he found himself caught up in the middle of an uprising led by Cunedda Wledig and Urien Rheged against the Irish who had settled in west Wales. A woman approached him, but her advances were rejected; furious at being repulsed, she hired assassins to kill Brynach. Miraculously, they died horribly from lice and Brynach, his wounds now healed, travelled eastwards. The stages of his flight are marked by foundations dedicated to him: Llanboidy across the river Taf in Carmarthenshire; and, back in Pembrokeshire, Cilymaenllwyd and Llanfyrnach, where he set up an oratory beside a spring before continuing on his journey to Henry's Moat and Pontfaen. He might have settled at Pontfaen, having cleansed the place of evil spirits, but the nights were made hideous and unbearable by their cries and he was forced to move to Cwm-yr-Eglwys and finally to Nevern. Here, a white sow and her piglets led him to where his church should be built on the banks of the Gaman and his mission began. An early convert to Brynach's teaching was Clethyr, who, though an old man, departed as a missionary to St Clear's in Cornwall. Brynach demonstrated powers over men and wild animals. Stags pulled his cart; his cow was herded by a wolf; and when Maelgwn Gwynedd stole it to feed his followers, no fire burned with heat to cook it. Maelgwn recognised his sin and was overcome by Brynach's hospitality. Eventually, so many people became disciples of the saint that he sought refuge in a cave on Carn Ingli – the Mount of Angels – above Nevern, where he would converse with divine messengers.

squinch; one theory suggests that such spaces formed a sort of cell for an eremitic priest. The church has a square font (unusual in Pembrokeshire) and at one time housed three stone altars which had been brought here from Pill Priory. The existing building dates from 1670. The living does not seem to have prospered, since towards the end of that century a report stated that there was no glebeland attached

St Brynach's, Pontfaen in 1859, showing the altars from Pill Priory

to it and that the church showed signs of having been neglected. By 1859, the church was described as 'ruined with all three altars remaining within the abandoned walls and its font open to all the birds of heaven'. It was fortunate that Pontfaen house, beside the church, was owned at that time by the Gower family of Castle Maelgwyn; Mrs Gower, at her own expense, installed new windows of Bath stone in the church and had them glazed in green glass. When the Gowers sold out in 1863 to Richard Arden, a lawyer from London, he and his family continued the refurbishment of the church: his son Percy Arden added a porch and vestry between 1905 and 1907 and presented Pontfaen with a very fine set of embroidered vestments. This level of care continued throughout the 20th century and several generations of the Reed family of Tŷ Gwyn farm in the valley have served as church wardens, maintaining the building like a jewel in its dramatic setting.

There are two early memorial stones in the churchyard to the right of the path. At the beginning of the 20th century the one inscribed with a Latin

St Brynach's in 2002, interior

cross had fallen over, and the other, decorated with a wheel-cross, was acting as a gatepost; the former was re-installed and the latter set up close to it. Both are 7th–9th century in date.

LLANSTINAN CHURCH (ST JUSTINIAN)   OS SM 954 338

From the church at Pontfaen, the route climbs further up the hill to join the B4313 and turns right towards Fishguard. On reaching the crossroads north of Llanychaer church, follow the road signposted to Trecŵn, which takes the pilgrim along a minor road for nearly 3.5ml, over the ridge dividing the Gwaun river catchment from that of the Western Cleddau or Cleddau Wen. The river rises at Ffynnon Cleddau on a farm to the left of the road called Llygad-y-Cleddau, the Cleddau's Eye. At the A40 junction, a right turn leads downhill, and at the end of a straight section a signpost on the right indicates the way up to Llanstinan church.

Although it is an ancient highway through to Fishguard, the lane leading towards the church is rough, so for some car pilgrims it may be preferable to park in one of the two lay-bys near the turning and make the 0.6ml journey on foot. This old road skirts an ancient lakebed formed by the run-off from melting ice at the end of the Last Glaciation. It extends downstream for nearly 3.5ml, and in the early 17th century, George Owen in his *Description of Penbrokshire* enthused about the great numbers of eels and lampreys to be taken from it during the month of August, listing crane, spoonbill and bittern as well as duck, teal and heron as common in these bogs. Duck and teal are still common, heron too, though now no longer considered a culinary delicacy. Despite the canalisation of the river in the 18th century and the felling of trees for pit and trench props which continued into the 20th, this remained an area of reed, rush and willow carr into living memory.

Beside the little stream, Church Cottage retains on the road side a single curved corner to its outside wall – a feature of Pembrokeshire cottages. The curved corner is said to frustrate the devil looking for entry by preventing him from finding a fourth wall. Across the bridge over the stream, the path leads up to the elliptical, near circular, churchyard – a *llan* of pre-Christian origin and a sanctuary probably dating back to the Bronze Age. Llanstinan church nestles within this enclosure, shaded by trees of ash and lime. The ash tree is traditionally associated with sacred places. In Welsh and Breton, the name for the ash is *onnen* and in parts of Brittany it is linked with the cult of St Non, mother of St David.

Dedicated to St Justinian (also known as Stinan or Iestyn), friend and confessor to St David in the 6th century, the building is simple. The solid, uncluttered configuration of its walls and arches has a beauty which is at one with the surroundings of the church. Ferns

St Justinian's, Llanstinan, west end and bellcote

St Justinian's, Llanstinan

St Justinian's, interior

grow in the crevices of its walls and long-eared bats roost under the slates. Evidence of its early foundation may be seen in the west wall, below the bellcote. The first foundations, laid during pre-Conquest times, subsided, forming a hollow; later, medieval masons filled in the subsidence. Inside, the church comprises a nave and chancel with a south transept and squinch connecting it with the chancel. In the nave is a Norman font, and the windows are in the domestic style of the late 18th century; the current programme of restoration is installing exact copies. There are only two memorials in the church:

one commemorates the Revd Henry Miles and his wife who served the parish for thirty-eight years, and the other is unusual in that it is installed under the altar in the sanctuary. It is in memory of Fanny Owen, who died aged two months in January 1835. It would appear that she was a baby daughter of Sir John Owen of Orielton, who bought Llanstinan House in 1810 on the death of the previous owner, William Knox. William Knox's son, Thomas, held command of the Fishguard Fencibles during the French Invasion of 1797.

Outside, on the north side of the churchyard amid the entanglements of bracken and brambles, is a small two-roomed slate building which served until after 1877 as the school for the village which surrounded the churchyard. The foundations of a number of cottages are still discernible on the surface and the hedgerows which bound the plots sport rambler roses in August, even though the dwellings have almost disappeared.

Marked on George Owen's map as 'Lysclethe', this, however, was not the first settlement at Scleddau. On the hill to the south overlooking the church is an Iron Age site. It can be approached via the stile in the south-east corner of the churchyard, over the stream and up the hill. A well-marked ring and ditch, overgrown with blackthorn and bramble, indicate its position. There is a large standing stone at the eastern end. What events brought the hill settlers down to the valley is not known but a later move is more clearly understood. After 1793 the construction of the post-road from Fishguard to Haverfordwest brought changes to communities along the way. Gradually, people began to move away from the site of the church to the crossroads in the present village. What is now the Gate Inn collected the tolls that caused such unrest elsewhere across the county during the Rebecca Riots of the 1830s.

The pilgrim route avoids the present village of Scleddau. A left turn back onto the A40 and the first right turn off it, brings the traveller along a causeway above the bog and to a bridge over the Cleddau which has been in use possibly since Neolithic times.

The causeway is constructed of huge Preseli boulders, interlocking with each other and rising and falling with the water levels in the marsh or lake-bed beneath. The bridge is of corbelled construction with nine capstones, each over two metres in length. In the centre, the widest is 1.5m broad, suggesting that the original packhorse bridge was later extended to accommodate wheeled traffic. In the 4,000 years or so of use, smaller stones and layers of water macadam have been added by generations of road menders to build up the carriageway, until in the 19th century culm and rubble with fragments of pottery became incorporated in the fill and parapets were added. This ancient road

Prehistoric bridge over the Cleddau, Llanstinan

continues up the hill, marked until recently by a Bronze Age burial mound, past the school which took over from the establishment in Llanstinan churchyard, and bears left onto the old road from Fishguard to St Davids in the direction of Mathry.

From either Granston (Route A) or Llanstinan (Route B), the way to Mathry is along the A487 as far as the crossroads with the B4331, where a right turn leads uphill to the centre of the village.

Mathry church

The hilltop village of Mathry has claims to be one of the oldest in Pembrokeshire. The field boundaries can be seen to radiate down the contours from the central square, on which stands the church. The present building of 1869 is the fifth church on the site and was intended to carry a spire, but funds ran out before this was achieved. It stands high on a mound above the thoroughfares, with a large nave and semi-octagonal chancel. During the 19th-century rebuilding, a vestry was added on the north side of the chancel and a porch on the south-west end of the nave. The interior is open and surprisingly modern in concept. Tall columns frame the chancel and neither pulpit nor dark pews interrupt the sense of space. Light from the east windows concentrates from every angle onto the altar.

The derivation of the name Mathry and the dedication of

Mathry, interior

the church are not entirely clear, but the most attractive account is that of the 12th-century *Liber Landavensis*, the *Book of Llandaff*. It describes how St Teilo, walking beside the river Taf at Llanddowror, rescued seven baby boys, whose father was about to drown them, since he was too poor to provide nourishment for them. The saint baptised them and each day they received fish from the river to eat.

Seven Martyrs badge (Mathry V.C. School)

Eventually they were sent to Mathry where, known as the seven saints, they spent the rest of their lives. In the 17th and 18th centuries, a number of cist burials were discovered near the churchyard and these were immediately dubbed 'the coffins of the Martyrs'. More recently, other cist graves were found near the car park and public conveniences; Rhoslanog farm, 1ml to the west, may be the site of an early Christian cemetery. Recovered from the wall of Rhoslanog farmhouse, a stone inscribed with a wheel-cross is now one of two built into the west wall of the churchyard. The second was found serving as a gatepost at Tregidreg farm, to the south of the A487. Both probably belong to the 9th century.

A stone in the church porch belongs to an earlier period,

Wheel-cross, Mathry churchyard wall

probably the 5th or 6th century. It was recorded in 1698 by Edward Lhuyd in the course of his researches for the 1707 edition of William Camden's *Britannia*. After this, the stone was lost until rediscovered in 1937 planted upside down and used as a gatepost at the western entrance to the churchyard. The inscription is cut in Ogham and Latin scripts and reads: 'Mac Cudiccl son of Caticuus [lies here]'. The 'MAC' is now missing. Some scholars have suggested that the word forms used here are more similar to Irish than to contemporary Welsh forms, which accords with the Ogham inscription and with the curious inverted form of the letter S, which is not common. Near the altar lies another carved stone. The cross is carved in relief, and the letters α and Ω – Alpha and Omega – are inscribed above the arms; beneath them appear the letters 'IHC'. It is unusual to find these symbols on early stones; this stone probably dates from the 10th or 11th century. It has had a curious recent history. It was known to be at St Edrin's church near Llandeloy before the building became a private house. It then disappeared and was rediscovered in the late 1980s lying beside the coast path, whence it was taken to Mathry for safekeeping.

Mathry was an important benefice of the diocese in medieval times. A prebendary, it was held in the 12th century by Giraldus Cambrensis, though not without a running conflict between him and Bishop Peter de Leia. Mathry was also substantial enough to be granted a market and hiring fair by King Edward III. Though the market had been abolished by 1810, the fair continued into the 20th century.

A diversion from the pilgrim route towards the coast at this point gives the pilgrim the opportunity of viewing the impressive Carreg Samson cromlech.

From Mathry, take the right-hand turn to Abercastle (2.3ml), bearing right at the fork and proceeding across the crossroads down into the picturesque coastal village. At Abercastle, take the road left to Trefin for 0.3ml and park outside Longhouse farm. Walk down the lane towards the farmhouse; Carreg Samson is located in a field along a track to the right of the farm.

A more dramatic location for a 4th–early 3rd millennium BC burial chamber is difficult to imagine. In an exposed position overlooking Abercastle Harbour and the rocky promontories towards Strumble Head, the impressive cromlech looks like a lumbering dinosaur emerging up the slope from the sea. It comprises six uprights (originally seven), three of which support the massive capstone. Excavations in

Carreg Samson burial chamber

1968 unearthed shards of pottery which held cremated bone. Interestingly, the chamber was discovered to have been erected in a pit, which suggests that the twelve-ton capstone may have been a naturally occurring erratic, already on site, which the enterprising Neolithic engineers dug out and hoisted onto the uprights. Legend has it that St Samson performed the operation with his little finger (and severed it in the process): the tomb was once known as the Grave of Samson's Finger.

St Samson (485–565)

Feast Day: 28 July

The story of this saint survives in a number of Lives. Born in Glamorgan, the son of the Breton Amwn Ddu ('The Black') and Anna, a daughter of Meurig ap Tewdrig from Gwent, Samson studied under St Illtud at the great seat of learning at Llanilltyd Fawr (Llantwit Major), Glamorgan, and is supposed to have been ordained by St Dyfrig (Dubricius). His mission took him to Ynys Bŷr (Caldey Island, where he was abbot); Ireland; 'desert regions' near Stackpole and Bosherston in south Pembrokeshire (where there is a Sampson Brake, a Sampson Cross and a Sampson farm); Cornwall; the Channel Islands; and, famously, Dol, south-east of St Malo in Brittany, where there are numerous dedications to the saint. At Dol, he founded a monastery and was named bishop; the magnificent 12th–13th century Cathedral there bears his name. Subsequent bishops of Dol held the status of archbishops of Brittany. Some genealogies identify Samson as the nephew of the historical Arthur, others as his cousin. In Wales, he is associated with feats of boulder-raising and throwing: witness the names of the burial chambers at Trellys near St Nicholas (Ffyst Samson) and at Abercastle (Carreg Samson). Although no Pembrokeshire churches are dedicated to him, three holy wells in the county (at Trenichol farm, north-west of Llandeloy; in the valley of the Eastern Cleddau near Llangolman; and in the parish of Newport) bear his name.

1ml south, overlooking the cove of Aberdraw to the west of Trefin – the site of an early palace of the bishops of St Davids – are the romantic ruins of an old corn mill, immortalised by William Williams ('Crwys', 1875–1968) in one of the best-known poems in Welsh.

From Trefin, the pilgrim can either proceed south on the coast road for 0.5ml into Llanrhian or rejoin the A487 just south of Square and Compass to view the decorated early Christian stone known as Mesur-y-Dorth.

The stone is located 0.75ml south of Square and Compass, set into the wall on the left by Maes-y-Garreg house.

The 7th–9th-century Christian stone known as Mesur-y-Dorth ('Measure of the Loaf') was presumably so called because its outline Latin ring-cross reminded local inhabitants of a round loaf cut into quarters. Its provenance is uncertain; it may have come from an early Christian cemetery in the vicinity. Tradition holds that St David decreed that the inscribed cross should serve as a template dictating the maximum size of a loaf in time of famine. It was at this spot during the Middle Ages that pilgrims travelling from the north are said to have eaten their final meal before entering St Davids, 6ml south. Another 9th–10th-century cross-inscribed stone in the area was also known as 'Mesur-y-Dorth' and was until the 1880s used as a gatepost at Penarthur farm, north of St Davids. Displaying a more elaborate outline wheel-cross of Irish derivation, it is known today as the Gurmarc stone (after the inscription on it), and is on display in the lapidarium situated in Porth y Tŵr (Tower Gate) over-looking St Davids Cathedral.

Mesur-y-Dorth stone

LLANRHIAN CHURCH (ST RHIAN)
OS SM 819 314

St Rhian badge
(Croesgoch C.P. School)

For pilgrims entering Llanrhian from Trefin, the church is located on the right-hand side of the road in the centre of the village. Those travelling south on the main A487 should turn right towards the coast at the crossroads in the centre of Croesgoch and proceed for 1ml into Llanrhian. Turn right at the crossroads on entering the village; the church is immediately on the left.

Located next to busy Manor farm and surrounded by a rookery, Llanrhian church stands on an ancient site. The curious stepped and pinnacled decoration on the squat saddleback

St Rhian (5th–6th century)
Feast Day: 8 March

St Rhian is said to have been one of St David's followers, but nothing certain is known about him and references to him are late. It has been suggested (unconvincingly) that he was Rein or Rhun, the son of Brychan Brycheiniog, or Reanus, a Welsh abbot. In all probability, however, one is dealing not with the personal name of an unknown saint but rather with a descriptive name comprising the elements *rhi* – 'king' – and *an* – a dimunitive ending, giving 'little king' and pointing, perhaps, to a local ruler who embraced Christianity.

Llanrhian church

tower is 19th century, though the body of the tower is 13th century, and may initially have been freestanding, serving as a refuge from sea-raiders. In 1418, the Archdeacon of Carmarthen, William Newport, who appointed priests to the living of Llanrhian, complained of the dilapidated state of the chancel, bemoaning the fact that it was his duty as Rector of Llanrhian to restore it. The original church had a double nave; it was rebuilt in its present cruciform shape in 1836 by the architect Daniel Evans. Further restoration was carried out in 1891, when the chancel screen, handsome oak pews and ceilings were installed. The rebuilding has resulted in a formal-looking, plain and spacious interior lined with dark pine panelling that is rather at odds with the architectural quirkiness and character of the exterior. The carved oak altar was given to the church in 1942 by the vicar, Canon R. Keeble-Williams and his family, in memory of their son who died in India in the Second World War.

The striking white decagonal font dates from the 15th century. It features ten plain, inverted shields. One of these bears the arms of the great Tudor nobleman and powerful supporter of Henry VII, Sir Rhys ap Thomas (1449–1525) – a chevron surrounded by three ravens. (Though the shield is inverted, the heraldic device is not.) Rhys ap Thomas played a central role in the events leading up to the Battle of Bosworth in 1485 and remained Henry VII's trusted ally. It is said that Rhys brought the stone or partly made font back from Jerusalem to Carmarthen, from where it found its way here.

Font, Llanrhian

Two decorated stones have been built into the north-west wall of the nave near the tower. At ground level is a very rough 7th–9th-century slab incised with a wheel-cross. The second stone, dating from the 8th century, is at about chest height and is inscribed with a tiny consecration cross within a circle. A number of consecration crosses – both inside and outside – were carved or painted on the walls of early churches and often anointed with oil at the consecration ceremony.

Lying 0.6ml north of Llanrhian is the popular harbour village of Porthgain, dominated on one side of the quay by the dramatic, jagged ruins of the demolished slate and brick works.

Continue south from Llanrhian on the minor coast road past the turnings for Portheiddi and Abereiddi (the site of the beautiful Blue Lagoon and of ghostly vestiges of the slate industry) into Cwmwdig Water.

Cwmwdig farm, 0.6ml south-east (OS SM 805 301; no access since this is private land) was once the site of a church or chapel. In the farmyard are the remains of the holy well with which the chapel was associated. In 1715, the antiquary Browne Willis noted that he had been reliably informed that people were still coming to 'bathe in the chapel well' during the 17th century, at which time it was 'arched over'. A portion of the arch is still visible, as are the steps leading down to the well.

At this point, the pilgrim journeying towards St Davids enters Cylch Dewi – The Sacred Landscape of St David (p. 103).

IN THE SHADOW OF THE PRESELIS

The trackways along the spine of the Preseli mountains have been used by travellers, traders, invaders and pilgrims ever since the first farmers began to cultivate the thin but fertile upland soils during the Neolithic period, around 5,000 years ago. It was from Carn Meini (also known as Carn Menyn – 'The Cairn of Butter' – possibly a reference to the rich pasture-land in the area) and along these tracks that the Preseli dolorite, the bluestone, was transported to Stonehenge in Wiltshire – an epic feat of prehistoric engineering. Because of their command over the Preseli mountains, the leaders of the Iron Age and the early Christian settlers were able to exercise control over the farmland nestling in the shadow of impressive cairns and hillforts such as Foel Drygarn. The area is rich in history and archaeology; it also abounds in legend, Christian and pagan. It was across this particular landscape that King Arthur is supposed to have pursued the fierce boar, Twrch Trwyth, in the legend of Culhwch and Olwen; the cult of St Teilo flourished here, his skull, worn smooth by centuries of use, being used by pilgrims to scoop healing water out of his holy well; it was to this locality that St Brynach fled from physical and spiritual persecution; and in the Middle Ages, these mountains became a focus for the struggle between the native Welsh princes and the Norman invaders.

In the Shadow of the Preselis

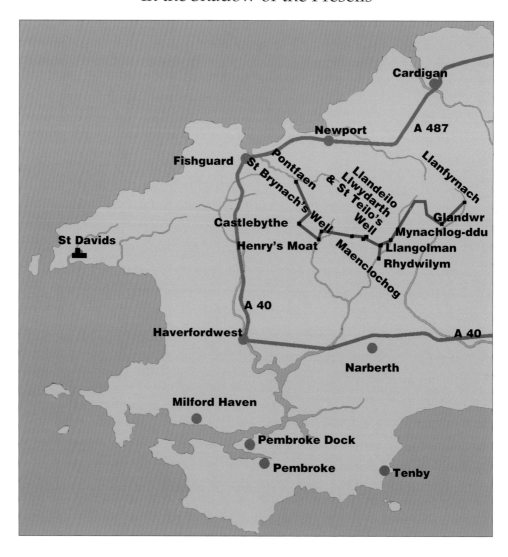

The first church on this site was probably founded in the 12th century when the *Ecclesia Sancti Bernachi de Blaentav in Kemeys* – the church of St Brynach at the source of the river Taf in the hundred of Cemais – was given to the Knights Hospitallers of St John of Jerusalem, together with 100 acres of agricultural

St Brynach's, Llanfyrnach
(*photo:* Edward Perkins)

land, by Stephen, Constable of Cardigan Castle and son-in-law to Rhys ap Tewdwr, King of Deheubarth. Rebuilt in 1842 using slate from the quarries at Glogue to the north, the church stands on a raised circular mound surrounded by a slight embankment and precipitous ditch on the east and south sides. To the north-west rises the mound of a medieval castle motte, and the church seems to be located in the bailey. Well-stocked fishponds were a medieval feature of the valley below. The dark, solid tower is squat and pinnacled. There are some attractive finials to the roof and the

Rhyd-y-Gath stone

Efessangus stone, Glandwr

windows are a mixture of Gothic and Tudor styles. The rectangular nave is simple and sparse, and the font, on which are engraved the letters T.D., is of Norman type.

A short distance west at Rhyd-y-Gath ('the wild cat's ford'; OS SN 215 312), resting against a field boundary opposite a modern barn at the entrance to the farm, is a 7th–9th-century Christian stone incised with a Latin ring-cross. Another stone bearing the legend 'TAVUS', now lost, was once located here. Just over 2ml south-west at Glandwr (OS SN 191 286), near the gate of a fine Baptist chapel founded in 1712, stands another stone dating from the 5th or 6th century whose Ogham dedication reads 'EFESSANGUS ASEGNUS'. The stone is super-inscribed with a 7th–9th-century Latin wheel-cross on a tripod base.

From Glandwr, take the steep road that rejoins the A478 just south of Pentre Galar. Just beyond the village, turn left onto the unfenced mountain road towards the Preseli range.

For pilgrims arriving in the village along the mountain road which crosses the shoulder of Foel Drych from Pentre Galar, the view across to Foel Drygarn, Carn Meini, Foel Cwm Cerwyn and, in fine weather, beyond them to the sea, is spectacular. Legend and folk memory live on in this land of rock and moorland. Travelling through the village of Mynachlog-ddu, several monuments will focus the attention of the pilgrim on different aspects of its past. Turning right at the junction at the bottom of the hill, it is worth stopping at Bethel Baptist chapel, on the right-hand side of the road (OS SN 145 304).

The original 1794 chapel survives as the adjoining schoolroom. The present building was erected in 1875–77, and has especially fine plaster-work on the ceiling. However, its most notable monument is in the churchyard, against the east wall: the grave of Thomas Rees (1806–76). Nicknamed 'Twm Carnabwth' after his farm, he achieved fame by taking part in the first attack on the toll gate at Efailwen on the Narberth to Cardigan road, now the A478, on 1 May 1839. Such was the agrarian unrest and social disquiet at the time that this was followed 13 days later by riots in Carmarthen which spread across west Wales. The rioters adopted the name 'Rebecca' from a passage in Genesis 24, donned women's clothing and blackened their

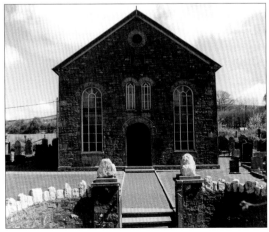

Bethel chapel, Mynachlog-ddu

faces – disguises which derived from an old folk custom called Y Ceffyl Pren (The Wooden Horse). West of the chapel after 0.6ml, on the common of Rhos Fach, is the impressive memorial stone to the great Welsh poet, pacifist, mystic and Quaker Waldo Williams (1904–71). The inscription, which refers to the mountains overlooking the common, is taken from one of his best-known poems, 'Preseli'; the translation runs: 'The wall of my boyhood: Foel Drigarn, Carn Gyfrwy, Tal Mynydd,/ At my back in all independence of mind'.

Twm Carnabwth's gravestone, Bethel chapel

St Dogmael's church lies 1.6ml south of the village on the route signposted to Maenclochog. 0.8ml along the road, a notice marks a gateway giving access to the prehistoric stone circle of Gors Fawr.

Gors Fawr stone circle

The Gors Fawr circle, 21 metres in diameter, consists of 16 stones standing up to 1m high, guarded to the north-east by two standing stones 2m in height. Overlooked by the jagged outline of Carn Meini, this is just one of the many

Neolithic and later-prehistoric ritual, occupational and burial sites on the slopes of the Preselis.

St Dogmael's church, a short distance further on, is situated on an elliptical platform above Afon Wern, a tempestuous tributary of the Cleddau Ddu. Originally it was the chapel of a manor owned by the Tironian order of the Black Monks of St Dogmael's Abbey, near Cardigan, a designation from which Mynachlog-ddu may derive its name. It appears in the *Taxatio* of 1291 as the *Capella de Nigra Grangea.*

St Dogmael's church

However, there may be an earlier dedication to St Egidius or St Giles, known in Welsh as Sant Silin. This attribution, recorded by George Owen, is consistent with the name of a pilgrim chapel he noted in the vicinity – Capel Silin or Capel Bach to the north-west, probably near Mynydd Bach, of which no trace survives. Owen also recorded another chapel called Capel Cawy, 2ml to the north-east (marked on OS maps as Fferm-y-Capel). The farm named Llandre, uphill and to the east of the church, has buildings of considerable antiquity, the foundations of which are likely to be part of the original monastic grange.

At the Reformation, patronage of the benefice of St Dogmael's passed into the hands of the Phillips family of Picton and remained with them until the Church in Wales was disestablished in 1922.

The present building is a two-celled medieval church. It consists of two aisles, each with a three-bayed nave continous with the chancel with no structural division between them. The north aisle, which is the longer, is probably the earlier of the two (possibly 14th century in date), and the door in the north wall belongs to this period. The south aisle appears to be late 15th century and the three-bay arcade supported on octagonal piers is of this period. The west doorway is different from that on the north side, but it probably also dates from the 15th century. There is no chancel arch in either cell. Though later rebuilt, the bellcote was probably in place during the Middle Ages. The font is medieval on a modern base.

Little extensive alteration to the church is recorded until in 1888 an application was submitted for major reconstruction. This was refused, but in 1889 restoration work did take place. Most of the medieval elements were retained but both aisles were re-roofed, the bellcote rebuilt, the windows throughout the church replaced and the seating capacity increased to accommodate 120. The cost of the work came to £800. The church was closed for 6 years during the 1980s, but the efforts of the then Cleric in Charge, the Revd Anthony Bailey, together with local support and fund-raising activities, ensured that it was reopened in 1988 – an event heralded by a candlelit midnight service in the absence of electricity on Christmas Eve, 1987.

Continue for 0.6ml to the next junction, where a left turn leads downhill into the valley. At the junction, turn right and pass though the village of Llangolman. After a further 0.6ml, turn left, following the signs for Rhydwilym and Llanycefn. Llangolman church stands 200m along this road on the right.

Located in a raised circular churchyard on high ground above a supposed Roman road from Llanglydwen to Maenclochog and commanding magnificent views over the lush wooded valley of the Eastern Cleddau or Cleddau Ddu, the tiny church of Llangolman had by the end of the 19th century fallen into total disrepair. Local tradition holds that it was restored by a farmer who wanted to use it

Capel Colman Waymarker

St Colman (6th century)
Feast Day: 20 November

There are so many Irish saints named Colman that it is difficult to say with any certainty to which one the churches at Llangolman and at Capel Colman near Boncath are dedicated. It has been suggested that the likely candidate is the Colman who founded the see of Dromore and became its bishop. He is said to have studied under St Elvis or Elfyw and to have journeyed thrice to Rome, where he was consecrated bishop by Pope Gregory. On a visit to Wales, he is credited with the miracle of restoring to life a still-born child – no less a figure than the future St David – whom he then educated. Serving as a gatepost near the church at Capel Colman is a reused prehistoric pillar-stone known as Maen-ar-Golman which is said to be the saint's gravestone.

49

St Colman's, Llangolman

Martha Thomas's gravestone, Llangolman

as the setting for his daughter's wedding. Inside, the church comprises a simple nave and chancel, on the south wall of which is an interesting monument to Stephen Lewis of Llangolman who died in 1728: 'Such seed as in this present life men sow/Such shall they reap when God says come & go'. In the churchyard is a gravestone to the memory of Martha Thomas of Pomprenmaen who died on Valentine's Day 1820, aged 43. Local tradition holds that she was a great provider of home brew – and, it seems, other services – to the local gentry. Appropriately, a wine glass heads her tombstone.

Rhydwilym Baptist Chapel
OS SN 114 248

Before proceeding west to Llandeilo Llwydarth, it is worth descending the steep 1.4ml route into the valley to visit Rhydwilym chapel.

Rhydwilym chapel

Rhydwilym is the fine mother-church of the Baptists of west Wales, incorporated in 1668. This is a serene and atmospheric place. It was in the Eastern Cleddau, which flows past Rhydwilym, that the congregation was once baptised. There is now a baptistery pool to the north of the chapel. In the cemetery behind the chapel is the grave and monument of John Evans (died 1705), who built the first formal chapel here in 1701 – 'the newly-built slate-house' as it was known, to distinguish it from nearby thatched houses. It would have been much

John Evans's monument, Rhydwilym

smaller than the present structure, with small windows to avoid the Window Tax. In the evening, it would have been lit by rush candles. This is a chapel with a distinguished history: in past centuries, members of the congregation walked here from Newport in north Pembrokeshire and from as far afield as Swansea. In 1939, Waldo Williams paid tribute to the resilience of the early Baptists of Rhydwilym during periods of great religious persecution: 'The proof of their greatness was the definitiveness with which they rejected the interference of the State.'

The pilgrim now retraces the journey up the valley, bearing left at the junction beyond Llangolman church. A turning to the left, 1.5ml along the minor road from Llangolman to Maenclochog, brings the pilgrim to the ruins of this little church. It lies behind Llandeilo farm but access is clearly marked. For walkers, there is an alternative route from Llangolman church. Continue south for 0.3ml, turning right to Llangolman farm. For 1ml, the bridle path follows a green road as it gently descends through woods along a sunken way with hollows and glades carpeted in moss and spurge. Fragile wood anemones light the banks. At the ford, ruined walls, ponds, gooseberry bushes and an enclosure indicate the site of old mills. The way climbs again to Llandeilo Llwydarth, sometimes becoming a stream bed as water flows into it from St Teilo's Well. Strong waterproof footwear is recommended.

The last entry in the baptismal register of St Teilo's church was in 1860. In 1897 it was roofless and the chancel arch was likely to 'fall at any moment'. It is a small rectangular building, the nave being 17 x 14 feet and the chancel 12 x 10 feet, with a stone bench still visible around the walls of the nave. One service is held here each year on a fifth Sunday of the month during the summer.

This site is closely tied to the early Christian traditions of north Pembrokeshire. Not

Ruins of St Teilo's, Llandeilo Llwydarth
(*photo:* Edward Perkins)

St Teilo or St Eliud (6th century)   Feast Day: 9 February

The accounts of the life of St Teilo state that he was born at 'Eglwys Gunniau' – probably Penally, near Tenby – studied under Dubricius, possibly on Caldey, and was, with St David, a pupil of Paulinus, remaining with David during the foundation of his monastery in the Vallis Rosina. He accompanied David and Padarn to Jerusalem and succeeded Oudoceus as episcopal abbot at the monastery of Llandaff. In the year 547, yellow plague broke out in south Wales and Teilo along with many others fled first to Cornwall and then to Brittany. He was welcomed in Brittany by Budic, King of the province of Cornouaille. He spent seven years at Dol, fraternising with St Samson who had been a contemporary of his at the monastery on Caldey. Together they planted an orchard three miles long south of the town. Before returning to Wales, he killed the obligatory monstrous serpent. The story of his rescuing seven little boys from drowning in the Taf is a legend which brings the foundations of Llanddowror and Mathry (dedicated to the seven 'Holy Martyrs') under the influence and protection of this important saintly figure. When he eventually died at Llandeilo Fawr in Carmarthenshire, there was some dispute as to where his body should be laid to rest. It was claimed by Penally as his birthplace, by Llandaff as his place of ministry and by Llandeilo Fawr as his final residence. Miraculously, overnight, the body presented itself in triplicate, solving the dilemma. The skull, Penglog Teilo, has a separate history spanning 1,500 years and was for a time closely linked to the little church of Llandeilo Llwydarth in Pembrokeshire and with the cure of respiratory diseases at his well nearby. There are many dedications to St Teilo and associations with him in south Wales, especially in Pembrokeshire, and in Brittany, where he is considered the patron saint of horses and apple trees and his aid invoked in the treatment of fevers.

only is it dedicated to St Teilo, who was born in Pembrokeshire at Penally near Tenby, but it is associated with the cult of the saint's skull – Penglog Teilo. Three 5th or 6th-century memorial stones were found in the churchyard and at a nearby property, recording three generations of the same family. The grandfather, Cavetus, has no memorial, but his name is quoted on the stones of his sons Coimagnus, whose stone was found beside a stile leading into the churchyard, and Andagellus, whose stone was discovered outside the chancel at the east end. Andagellus had a son, Curcagnus; his stone may have been erected originally in the churchyard, but it was

Service at St Teilo's, Llandeilo Llwydarth

found serving as a gatepost at the entrance to the nearby farm of Temple Druid. In 1896 it was removed on the orders of Lord Cawdor to the churchyard at Cenarth, where it has remained. The Coimagnus and Andagellus stones are now under the tower in Maenclochog church where they have been placed for safekeeping. On each the Latin script is rough but clear: 'COIMAGNI FILI CAVETI', 'ANDAGELLI IACIT FILI CAVETI' and 'CURCAGNI FILI ANDAGELL'; on the Andagellus stone the Ogham script reads 'ANDAGELLI MACU CAV', using the Irish form 'macu' for 'son', rather than the Latin 'fili'. Later, a linear Latin cross with trifid terminals was inscribed above the lettering. A famous photograph of 1898 shows Mrs Melchior, the custodian of St Teilo's Skull at the time, resting it on the Coimagnus stone. At the east end of the ruined church the gravestones of two members of the Melchior family remain: Thomas Melchior, who died on 26 October 1821, aged 29, and his daughter Emmy Catherine, who died on 20 August 1835.

Archaeological aerial photography has shown that the circle of the churchyard is enclosed within a larger defensive bank and ditch which also bound the farms of

Memorial stones of Cavetus family

Prisk and Temple Druid, previously called Bwlch-y-Clawdd. The earlier name, meaning 'the breach in the bank', may derive from the defensive enclosure. A yeoman house existed here from the 15th century. It was rebuilt in the 1790s by the architect John Nash for Henry Bulkeley and the name changed to Temple Druid. There are a number of sites in west Wales which have defensive enclosures around the church and surrounding hamlet. They are difficult to date, but most are associated with prehistoric settlements and burials, and with early Christian stones.

ST TEILO'S WELL   OS SN 101 270

Retracing one's steps back a short distance along the road in the direction of Llangolman, one reaches a footpath across a field on the right, opposite a house called Maenteilo. The well is located beyond the hedge boundary at the lower end of the field.

Water gushes out from the ground and flows past a series of crude, stone-built pools which are on occasion filled with water. It is

Pool structures, St Teilo's Well, Llandeilo Llwydarth

not entirely clear whether all these structures are associated with the cult of St Teilo. They are comparable in size, if not in architectural quality, to the immersion pools found at Holywell in Clwyd, at Ffynnon Gybi on Anglesey, and to others in

Frontispiece, Mary
Melchior's Bible, 1794

Penglog Teilo (St Teilo's Skull)

The legend of the skull begins with the saint on his deathbed instructing his maidservant to take it, one year after burial, to her home, where it would prove a blessing. Some time later, the responsibility for the care of St Teilo's tomb at Llandaff was placed in the hands of a guardian family, passing in due course to the Mathews family. In 1403, the cathedral and tomb were desecrated by pirates, but the tomb was restored in the 15th century by its keeper, Sir David Mathews, in recognition of which he was rewarded with the gift of what was claimed to be the skull of the saint. Anatomically and chronologically, its authenticity is unlikely, but there is no doubting the veneration in which it was held and the strength of belief in its power. The relic remained with the Mathews family for seven generations until 1658, when it was passed to the Melchiors at Llandeilo Llwydarth on the understanding that it would return to some branch of the Mathews family if there was no male Melchior to inherit. It was used as a drinking vessel to scoop water from the well. Although the Melchior guardian expressed scepticism when interviewed by members of the Cambrian Archaeological Society during a visit in 1897, many claimed to have been cured by it. The skull was sold back to the Mathews family in 1927 for £50. After this it was traced to Hampshire and then seems to have disappeared. In 1993, an article in the *Sydney Herald* told how it had been passed down the family to Captain Robert Mathews, who on 9 February 1994 brought it back to Llandaff.

Cornwall and Brittany. It was here that St Teilo's Skull exercised its healing powers. The water, drunk from the skull, was believed to be beneficial for whooping cough and all manner of chest complaints.

St Non's Well, Dirinon, Brittany

The route continues west for 0.8ml into Maenclochog, where a left turn at the junction brings the pilgrim into the centre of the village.

Maenclochog – 'The Ringing Stones' – is said to take its name from the two large stones which used to stand beside Ffynnon Fair (St Mary's Well), 0.5ml south-west of the village beside the road to Llys-y-frân.

Although there has been a church on the site since the time of the

St Mary's, Maenclochog

Norman incursions, no trace of it survives, except for the plain square font which may date from the 13th century. In the 1790s, it was rebuilt entirely by subscription. At that time it had a simple two-bayed nave and chancel with neo-gothic arches, a south transept and a triple-decker pulpit. The crenellated west turret was built partially into the nave structure and carried a gothic-style belfry. Entrance to the church – as at present – was through the ground floor of the tower.

Extensive restoration was again undertaken in 1881 to the specifications of the architects Middleton and Son of Westminster and Cheltenham, who added a vestry as a transept to the north, and moved the heating system from the south transept into the vestry. They also replaced the roofs and floors. This work, which cost £525, was mainly financed by Margaret Cropper, widow of Edward

Cropper, who built the Maenclochog railway through north Pembrokeshire, originally to carry slate from the quarries at Rosebush. The scheme prospered and became a tourist attraction. Cropper died in 1887 and the refurbishment of the church became part of his memorial.

Two memorials in the church record the change in the name and status of Bwlch-y-Clawdd farm near Llandeilo Llwydarth at the end of the 18th century. The earlier memorial, on the wall in the south transept, is to William Lewis and his wife of Bwlch-y-Clawdd. They left behind this injunction as their memorial:

> Behold by us you are but mortal men
> Still, pray, repent the hour you know not when.
> Death conquers all, both Knights, Lords, Dukes and Earls,
> They must depart and leave behind their pearls.
> Death of all worldley goods will men unvest,
> Then pray to God for Bliss and happy rest
> And earthly men in darkish room must lie.
> O then, prepare to God, for mercie crie
> And to true holiness your members give
> That after death in Heaven you may live.

The second, to Henry Bulkeley of Temple Druid who died in 1821, is on the south wall of the nave; it states, simply: 'There should be a tear for every one that dies.'

The Andagellus and Coimagnus stones from Llandeilo Llwydarth are placed under the tower on the south side of the church. These stones are witness to the existence of a strong community in this locality during the early Christian period, but there is no firm evidence of any pre-Conquest religious use of the site of the present church. After the arrival of the Normans, it belonged to the Deanery of Cemais and in 1291 the *Taxatio* valued the living at £6 13s 4d, of which a tenth was paid to the king. In 1320, with the two dependent chapelries of Llandeilo Llwydarth and Llangolman, it was granted as a valuable living to St Dogmael's Abbey by David De Rupe, Lord of the Manor of Maenclochog.

At the Reformation, it came into the possession of the Crown and, valued at £11 12s 11d, it was leased to John Leche of Llawhaden. In 1786, the benefice was united with Llangolman and Llandeilo Llwydarth – an arrangement formalised in the 19th century and continuing until 1998, when Henry's Moat, New Moat and Llys-y-Frân were added to the responsibilities of the vicar. After the Reformation there were further troubled times for the parish. In 1670, the Revd John Griffiths was censured by the bishop but his parishioners begged that he be kept on at least for the winter, rather than turned out in the cold. In 1743, a subsequent generation of churchwardens humbly requested the bishop to discharge their vicar, the Revd William Crowther, on 11 counts of negligence, drunkenness and lewd behaviour. At the end of the 18th century, social unrest and poverty beset the village, even though the cattle fair continued to be an important event in the county into the 20th century. In 1779, the Lord of Cemais, Lloyd of Bronwydd, attempted to withdraw the rights of turf cutters on the common – a right which was the main support of some of the poorest families. In 1795 there were bread riots, and the vicar intervened with the magistrates on behalf of his parishioners. In 1820, enclosures threatened their grazing rights on the common and then in 1839 came the increase in the levy of toll gate charges for local produce on its way to market. It was not surprising, then, that men from Maenclochog became involved in the

Rebecca Riots or that, later in the century when many had deserted the church and joined the nonconformist denominations, they protested against the levy of tithes they could not afford.

ST BRYNACH'S WELL   OS SN 054 280

From Maenclochog, proceed north-west along the B4313 towards Fishguard for 0.7ml, turning left at the first junction, signposted to Tufton. St Brynach's Well is located behind (lower) Bernard's Well farm, 1.5ml along this lane.

A footpath to the left of the lane leads down behind a barn that forms one side of the farmyard of the lower of the two farms named after the well. It is a living spring which flows out from beneath a stone arch into a rectangular well chamber. Slate steps, now out of alignment, descend to the water. Over the hedge on the west side there may have been a chapel; a pile of masonry is still visible, amongst which, in 1811, Richard Fenton saw a roughly incised stone cross. The well was renamed Bernard's Well at some point during the Norman period, possibly after the first Norman bishop of St Davids.

St Brynach's Well

Continue west for 0.6ml towards Tufton. Just before the junction with the B4329, a sharp left turn leads down to the church at Henry's Moat, which stands to the left of the lane opposite a large farm.

Though restored during the 19th century, some of the medieval fabric of the church is intact and it is possible that there may have been some pre-Conquest religious use of the site if the fragment of an early incised cross is in situ and has not been imported from elsewhere. The dedication to St Brynach

St Brynach's, Henry's Moat

suggests the existence of an earlier church, though the name was changed to Bernard and back again to Brynach in recent times.

In Welsh, the old name for the hamlet is Castell Hendre – 'the old settlement' – which illuminates the name of nearby New Moat, which was an episcopal manor prior to the Reformation. To the south of the churchyard, a single-bank settlement enclosure has been dated to the late Iron Age and in the field a little to the north-east there is an impressive 12th-century conical motte, over 20 feet high, which would have been surmounted by a wooden tower and defensive works. Now somewhat damaged around the base, it is clearly visible from the churchyard.

61

The church has been rebuilt several times. Initially, it was probably a cruciform structure consisting of nave, chancel and north and south transepts, with squinches or skew passages leading from both transepts to the chancel, all constructed during the 14th century. A corbel on either side of the chancel arch indicates the presence of a rood-loft at this time and the font – a square cushioned bowl on a cylindrical stem and square base – is 13th century in date.

The north transept seems to have been removed together with a squinch passage during the building work carried out in 1778. Further restoration took place in 1884–85, during which all openings from the nave – except the chancel arch – were blocked and a passage from the south transept was made to allow access to the new vestry. The roof was replaced and a polychrome tiled floor installed beneath a new seating plan in the nave and south transept. Most of the existing fittings, windows and pulpit belong to this restoration and at the same time the bellcote was rebuilt and a buttressed porch added on the north side of the nave. Most of this work was instigated and assiduously pursued by the then vicar, Thomas Mathias, who carried on a protracted correspondence with the bishop about every detail of the plans, including the need for a fireplace in the vestry, before his application to carry out the work was granted in 1884. Mathias continued to serve the parish until his death in 1907, when his parishioners commissioned the east window, depicting the resurrection, from the stained glass firm of J. Wippel and Son of Exeter. This was dedicated by the Archdeacon of St Davids on 12 November 1909.

Though now part of the Deanery of Daugleddau, in the post-Conquest period the church was in the Deanery of Cemais, and from 1488 the benefice was under private patronage and benefaction, which in the 19th century became that of the local squire. It was quite a valuable living, assessed in 1291 at £8 and at the time of the Reformation at £5 6s 8d. Between Henry's Moat and New Moat lies Farthing's Hook on the river Syfynwy at the head of Llys-y-Frân Reservoir. This farmstead, which also included fulling, corn and later woollen mills, became successively the property of important Pembrokeshire families: the Perrotts until 1548, the Scourfields of New Moat until 1627 and the Vaughans of Trecŵn and their descendants for over 300 years until 1939.

From Henry's Moat, the road to Pontfaen – where the Preselis trail links up with Route B of the Pilgrims from the Sea trail – crosses the B4329 at Tufton and enters Castlebythe, where the pilgrim may choose to follow the signs to Puncheston and Pontfaen. Alternatively, one can walk or drive over Castlebythe Mountain by taking a right turn at the crossroads in Castlebythe and proceeding towards Pontfaen on the B4313. From the highest point on this road it is possible on a clear day to see Carn Ingli above Newport, Garn Fawr on Pen Caer, Ramsey Island and St Ann's Head.

Before proceeding to Pontfaen, it is worth stopping briefly in Castlebythe to look at the disused church and the large medieval motte with its ditch filled by a spring.

The Bishop's Road

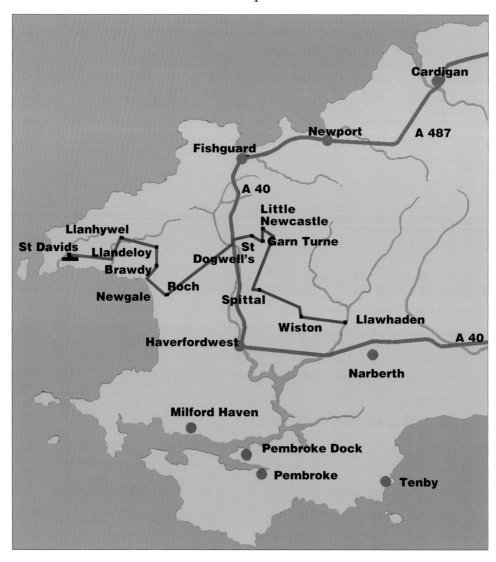

THE BISHOP'S ROAD

There is evidence that the route from Llawhaden to St Davids was in use before a castle was built at Llawhaden in the 12th century. The course of the Roman road to Carmarthen has been traced at least as far as Whitland, where it was discovered during excavations for the town's northern bypass, and aerial photography has shown that the road continued north of Wiston towards Spittal. In 1922, Sir Mortimer Wheeler made trial excavations of an enclosure which seemed to mark the site of a Roman marching camp known as Flemish Castle on the borders of the parishes of Ambleston and Castlebythe. The camp spans a route which leads in a direct line through Wolf's Castle in the direction of Roch. Apart from some Samian pottery, a flue and roof tiles, nothing was discovered that confirmed a Roman presence. Nevertheless, it was these roads that medieval pilgrims would have followed on their way westwards to the shrine, resting at hospices whose locations may be identified from place names. Having crossed the river Taf – at Llandeilo Abercowin perhaps – the pilgrim might rest at Whitland Abbey, Tavernspite, Llawhaden, Wiston, Spittal or Middle Mill between Llandeloy and Whitchurch, to arrive relatively refreshed at the Cathedral and the Palace re-built by Bishop Henry de Gower (1328–47).

The Bishop's Road follows the Landsker – the divide between Cymro-Norman and Welsh Pembrokeshire – and churches along the way are variously dedicated to saints favoured by the Norman settlers such as St Mary the Virgin, St Mary Magdalene and St Peter; other churches retained their dedications to saints of the early Welsh church such as St Aidan, St Dogfael and St Teilo.

The medieval diocese of St Davids was the largest and richest in Wales. Its authority covered the three counties of Dyfed as far north as Machynlleth, encompassing parts of Powys, the area north of Abergavenny and portions of Herefordshire as far east as Offa's Dyke. It gave the incumbent huge temporal and spiritual power. To fulfil his ministry and administrative duties it was necessary for the bishop to travel and in so doing provide accommodation for his entourage. Often he stayed at monastic institutions like Whitland or St Dogmael's but where there were large episcopal estates he built residences from which they could be controlled. At Llawhaden, the castle was primarily a stronghold erected on the boundary between the areas of Cymro-Norman settlement to the south and tribal Wales to the north. It is one of several episcopal residences in Pembrokeshire: other palaces were located at Lamphey outside Pembroke; St Davids, and Trefin, of which only traces of the fishponds remain.

The churches along the Bishop's Road vary in style, size and origin. Some are very simple with the nave, chancel and bellcote characteristic of north Pembrokeshire churches, while others show greater elaboration in their architecture, with features such as towers, transepts, arcaded aisles, chapels and vaulting. Almost all of them show signs of 19th or 20th-century restoration and additions, demonstrating their continued importance in the spiritual life of the community.

LLAWHADEN CHURCH (ST AIDAN)   OS SN 075 175

To arrive at Llawhaden, the motorist should follow the signpost at Canaston Bridge and turn off the A40 towards the village. At a distance of 1.1ml north of the main road, the way to the church forks off to the right and right again at the next junction, past the old mill. From the church, walkers who wish to visit the castle and hospital may take the footpath which climbs up into the village. Car pilgrims will need to retrace their route as far as the first fork; this is a sharp turn to the right.

Nestling in a dell under the shale cliffs cut by the Eastern Cleddau or Cleddau Ddu, the present church of St Aidan is an impressive and gracious building in a beautiful setting, its grounds bordered by the river. Its size is due to its episcopal associations. What we see today is a 14th-century reconstruction of an earlier foundation as witnessed by the dedication. In the records, the spelling of 'Aidan' varies, but this is probably the saint who was a pupil of St David and who became Bishop of Ferns, County Wexford, Ireland. He was also called Madoc or Maedoc, an appellation preserved in the name of a well near Whitesands beach, north-west of St Davids: Ffynnon Faiddog.

Bishop Ivor Rees and Bishop Huw Jones at St Aidan's, Llawhaden
(*photo:* Martin Cavaney)

St Aidan, Maedoc or Madoc (5th or 6th century)

Feast Day: 31 January

Born in Connacht, Ireland, St Aidan was one of many peregrinatory Irish saints whose religious mission led them across the sea to Britain and beyond. He came to Wales to study, first under St David's tutelage and subsequently under that of St Cennydd at his monastery on the Gower peninsula. Whilst with St David, he left a book out in the rain when he was called away to lead a team of timber-carrying oxen. The beasts fell over a precipice into the sea, but Aidan managed to save them, and returning to the place where he had left the book, found it whole and undamaged. In an alternative version of the tale, St David ordered Aidan to do penance for his carelessness over the book by lying prostrate on the shore at Whitesands Bay. As he did so, the tide rose and he was only saved from drowning by the intervention of St David. Returning to Ireland, he founded a monastery at Ferns in County Wexford and became its first bishop. His subsequent religious foundations in Ireland include Drumlane, County Cavan; Rossinver, County Leitrim; and Clonmore, County Carlow. He was noted for his interest in beekeeping and for his kindness and generosity to the poor. As a follower of St David, he lived on bread and water. In Pembrokeshire, the churches of Llawhaden and Solva are dedicated to St Aidan, whilst those at Haroldston West and Nolton are his under the name of St Madoc. Two wells – Ffynnon Faiddog near Whitesands and Ffynnon Madoc at Rudbaxton – also bear his name.

Remains of a 13th-century church exist in the chapel to the south of the chancel and the original squat tower, which in the 15th century was incorporated into a larger and much taller structure, gives the visitor the impression of a curious and complex edifice. There is a Norman font and the 14th-century nave and chancel are beautifully maintained. Access to the chapel is through an arcade and on the pillar capitals are carved patterns of twisted rope and double-headed animals, in a style found also on capitals at St Dogwell's. According to local tradition, a fine carved tomb in the chapel belonged to St Hugo. On the south wall of the nave is a memorial to William Evans who translated *Canwyll y Cymry* (*lit* 'the candle of the Welsh') – the

Animal whirligigs, Llawhaden

work of the famous 17th-century vicar Rhys Prichard – into English. The south doorway, access through which was blocked when the later tower was built, forms an archway on which is placed a tablet to one of the Owens of Henllys who was Chancellor of the Diocese of St Davids and Chaplain to Charles II. The east window was brought from Slebech church when it was sold and on the north side of the chancel arch is a boss on which is represented an animal whirligig of three hares whose ears meet at the centre. This carving is probably a 19th-century copy of the original and is a motif which occurs in other churches especially in Devon and Cornwall, where the beasts are known as 'The Tinner's Rabbits'. Another example can be seen in the roof just above the altar in the Lady Chapel in St Davids Cathedral. On the south side of the arch is a similarly designed trio of pelicans.

Outside at the east end, a degraded cross stone from the pre-Conquest period has been set into the wall. On its base may be seen traces of crosses inscribed by later pilgrims.

In 1862, the nave was largely rebuilt, the south doorway blocked and a porch added to the west end with some attractive gothic-style stone heads decorating the capitals supporting the arch.

A climb up the footpath, turning right at the top, leads to the castle. It is now the property of CADW and is open, free of charge, throughout the year.

High above the river, the first castle was built here in the 12th century by the first Norman bishop, Bernard, to protect his rich landholdings along the Eastern Cleddau and the famous forest of Llwydarth with its herds of red deer. At that time, the structure consisted of a circular ringwork of earth surmounted by timber and surrounded by a ditch, which is still visible. This protected the wooden buildings inside but was insufficient defence against

Llawhaden Castle, copper engraving by Sir Richard Colt Hoare, *c.* 1795

determined attack and was destroyed in 1192 by the Lord Rhys, Prince of Deheubarth. Around 1280, it was rebuilt in stone by Bishop Bec, who with his successor, Bishop David Martin, founded the borough of Llawhaden with its burgage plots, hospital and market. Later in the 14th century, the gatehouse was remodelled to create the imposing structure which remains, externally, almost intact to the present day.

Enormous powers lay in the hands of the bishop. The *Black Book of St Davids,* written for Bishop Martin in 1326, is a survey of all the lands, rents, dues and services paid to him at that time. He could punish crime, confiscate property and demand both payment for any transfer of tenure and compensation on the death of a tenant. Every third year he made claim on their productivity – a claim often paid in sheep, whose numbers varied according to the size of the holding. The services demanded by him as Lord of the Castle and Manor from the landholders at Llawhaden were diverse, ranging from agricultural work to the escort of prisoners. In addition, the *Black Book* records that 'if the Bishop in time of war should pass through his bishopric, they ought to follow him with the relics of the Blessed David as far as the town of Carmarthen'.

At the Reformation, Bishop Barlow stripped the lead from the roof and the interior fittings and further demolition took place in the 17th century. Early in the 20th century, the castle came into the care of the Pembrokeshire Association for the Preservation of Ancient Monuments, who carried out a great deal of conservation work by underpinning the walls and clearing the ivy.

At the western end of the village is a vaulted building – all that remains of Bishop Bec's hospital. It stands on high ground with a view which extends across the river and Minwear woods towards the south of the county. Inside the building an excellent display prepared by SPARC – the South Pembrokeshire Partnership for Action with Rural Communities – reconstructs the medieval life of the building and of those to whom it ministered.

The minor road past the hospice continues west towards Wiston – a pleasant route for walkers.

About 1.5ml west of Llawhaden and to the north of the lane lie Colby Moor and the farm of that name. Here in August 1645 during the Civil War, the Parliamentarians inflicted a massive defeat on the Royalists, despite the fact that the former had a comparatively tiny force to put into the field against the 150 horse, 1,100 infantry and field guns possessed by Charles I's troops. The Royalist losses were huge and 700 prisoners were taken. Within a week of the battle, Cromwell's commanders were in control of Haverfordwest and the surrounding area, having effected a public humiliation of the town. Even into the 19th century it was claimed that relics of the battle were still being turned up by the plough on this land.

WISTON CHURCH
(ST MARY MAGDALENE)
OS SN 022 180

A short distance beyond Colby Moor, a right turn uphill leads into the village of Wiston.

St Mary Magdalene's, Wiston

Founded by Wizo the Fleming, who was settled in the lordship of Daugleddau in the early 12th century, this is the only church in Pembrokeshire dedicated to St Mary Magdalene. In spring, the churchyard glows with amethyst and gold as crocus and daffodils break into flower between the graves and along the lime avenue leading to the low ogival arch of the 16th-century porch.

Renovation work in 1992 uncovered evidence which suggests that the tower was the first part of the church to be built around 1110 as a freestanding fortified structure 50 feet high. Access was through a doorway, now blocked, on the north side. Inside, a staircase leads to three upper levels which may have been habitable in times when the tower was used to defend the settlement. The nave and chancel are of 13th-century date, though the windows were replaced during renovations in 1864. The font is probably Norman and in the sanctuary a piscina and aumbry are also contemporary with the church.

Around 1145, Wizo's sons, Walter and Philip, gave the church to the Knights Hospitallers of Slebech, but this was contested by the Prior of Worcester and deeds in the cartulary at Gloucester indicate that their father had already signed to the convent there. The resulting dispute was sufficiently litigious to cause the king, Henry I, to intervene.

Memorials in the church include one on the south wall of the chancel to a member of the Wogan family, who took over Wiston through marriage early in the 14th century. The last male in the Wogan line, commemorated here, died in 1793, at which time the estate was bought by the Earl of Cawdor of Stackpole. In the centre of the south wall of the nave, a window by the stained glass designer Kempe of London depicting St George and St David was installed in 1920 as a parish memorial to those who had died in the First World War. Beneath the carpet at the west end of the nave is the Cawdor coat of arms.

Cawdor coat of arms

From the church there is a good view of the castle opposite. Access is through a gate into the field in which the castle and its bailey stand. The site was gifted by the Cawdor family to the nation in 1994 and is managed by CADW, who carried out excavations and consolidation in the castle and surrounding area in 1994.

The arrival of the Flemings at the beginning of the 12th century is recorded in a number of early historical accounts such as this from 1105:

'A great part of Flanders being drowned by the sea, the inhabitants were compelled to seek for some country to live in, their own being covered with water; and therefore, a great many being come over to England, they requested King Henry [Henry I, 1100–35] to assign them some part of his kingdom which was empty and void of inhabitants, where they might settle and plant themselves. The king, taking advantage of this charitable opportunity and being in manner assured that these Flemings would be a

Wizo's castle glimpsed behind St Mary Magdalene's church

considerable thorn in the side of the Welsh, bestowed on them very liberally what was not justly his to give and appointed them the county of Ros in Dyfed, west Wales.'

The Flemish enthusiastically pursued economic advancement and their promotion was part of the Norman plan for the cultural re-organisation of the county.

Thus the Gwis or Guise family arrived here, and Wizo was granted the Lordship of Daugleddau and built his castle on the site of what was probably a rath or Iron Age settlement. There are also indications that a road, thought to be Roman, ran some hundred yards to the north. Initially, the castle would have been a wooden tower surmounting the earth motte. The Welsh did not succumb quietly and being on the Landsker – the front line of the Welsh–Norman divide – the castle was attacked many times. In 1147 it was taken by Hywel ap Owen from Walter, Wizo's son, but the Flemish were soon back and held it until 1193 when it was again taken by the Welsh who were ousted once more two years later. It seems likely that the present polygonal shell keep was built soon after this event. Finally in 1220, Llywelyn ap Iorwerth attacked and destroyed the castle, and despite exhortations from King Henry III, repairs were never effected.

By the middle of the 13th century, the barony was in the hands of the Wogan family and passed out of them only in 1794 when it was sold to John Campbell, Lord Cawdor. The Wogan family built a manor which was developed into a large Tudor mansion on the site of the present manor house and the grounds became picturesque parkland including the ruins of the castle in its vistas.

The borough created by Wizo and his successors grew from a series of burgage plots inside the bailey and along its southern rim

Wiston manor house grounds and castle as seen in recent times

until, by the middle of the 13th century, there were narrow plots with dwellings all along the road and to the east of the castle and manor house. Excavations have shown that each plot covered an area of 855 square metres. Markets were held outside the churchyard and fragments of imported pottery discovered here point to a considerable level of prosperity among the burgesses. Despite a decline in the 14th and 15th centuries, not helped by an outbreak of the Black Death in 1348–49, the burgesses of Wiston were able in 1704 to claim the right to elect their own member of Parliament jointly with Tenby and Pembroke. It was a classic example of a Welsh 'rotten borough' and the inhabitants continued to elect their own mayor and aldermen into the 20th century. In the 17th century, Sir John Wogan MP was a strong Parliamentary supporter in the Civil War but it was his brother, Colonel Thomas Wogan, MP for Cardigan, who put his signature to the death warrant of Charles I. The 19th-century school building at the west end of the village is now used by the Wiston Project School which runs courses in furniture making. Behind it, the modern primary school is dedicated to St Aidan.

The way from Wiston to Spittal is not easy to follow without a map. Where the roads divide as one enters Wiston from the east, take the turning right (north) signposted to Clarbeston Road. About 2ml along the road, turn sharply right to arrive in the centre of Clarbeston Road. The route then crosses the railway and forks almost immediately left towards Walton East. After 0.75ml, a left turn is signposted to Spittal. This road passes the house and estate of Penty Parc and descends into the wooded valley of Cartlett brook, brilliant in spring when the young leaves dapple the bluebells with green and gold. Climbing again, the road crosses the B4329 Haverfordwest–Cardigan road just north of Scolton Manor and arrives outside the church in Spittal.

The village takes its name from the medieval *ysbyty* or *hospitium* founded by Bishop Bec in 1293 for the respite of pilgrims and the care of the sick. This was the property of St Davids Cathedral church, but it ceased to function at the Dissolution. Although no traces of it survive, it is thought to have occupied a site below the church and it has been suggested that the pile of stones used to build what is now Castle Cottage opposite the east end of the church may have been the remains of this building. A story tells how in 1572 three men discovered a brass pot full of gold and silver in the ruins of the hospice; however, both men and treasure disappeared without trace. After the Reformation, the living was held by the precentor of the Cathedral.

As recorded on a tablet set into its east side, the churchyard wall was rebuilt as a Millennium project. The foundations exposed at the base of the west wall of the church probably pre-date the present, mainly medieval, structure, which is similar in plan to many other north Pembrokeshire churches, lacking the defensive towers which characterise those on the Landsker.

On the north side are two curious features. The

St Mary's, Spittal

St Mary's, interior
(*photo:* Edward Perkins)

masonry outline of a blocked arch on the outside wall of the nave appears too wide to have been a doorway and it has been suggested that it might have formed part of a side chapel. A tomb in the churchyard projects right into the chancel wall and there are signs of disturbed masonry – perhaps the remains of an arch above it – whilst inside the chancel, a finished archway occupies the same position. This internal arch may represent a vestigial Easter Sepulchre; whatever the explanation, this is a curious coincidence of features.

On the south side, a lean-to vestry opens out of the chancel and a porch covers the door into the body of the church. There is a double bellcote at the west end and an external Sanctus or Priest's bell over the chancel arch. The nave is long and fairly narrow; the chancel is two-thirds of the length of the nave. The original chancel arch must have been quite low and narrow as squints on either side give a view of the altar from the body of the church. In the sanctuary, a piscina is incorporated into a south window sill. The font is Norman in style – square, with scalloped sides on a short cylindrical base.

Like many churches in the area, St Mary's has undergone periods of decline and restoration. In 1834, a distressed letter was sent by the then elderly vicar, the Revd Davies, to the Church Incorporated Building Society. It described how the church was 'full of pews and in every respect clean and decent and as full of congregation with their books in their hands answering the Minister' fifty years before when he had ministered to the parish. On his return to St Mary's as vicar half a century later, however, he discovered that 'there is now left but three rotten seats and four old benches throughout; the whole church . . . is equally disgraceful. I think that I can say without hesitation that there is no church in the Diocese, nor perhaps in the Kingdom, in so deplorable a condition as Spittal now is. When I meet the people going to the conventicles [chapels] on Sundays I cannot ask them in, for we have no place for them to sit down.' Though the correspondence, endorsed by the church wardens, continued into 1836, the Revd Davies eventually got his new seats and additional capacity.

Further major restoration was undertaken in 1897, when the chancel arch was widened and rebuilt, the handsome floor tiles and heating boiler installed, and many other improvements made. In

1992, the church was re-roofed, the work revealing much about previous structural changes and their consequent problems.

There are memorial tablets on the walls, many of them to members of the Higgon family of Scolton (now Scolton Manor Museum and Country Park), who were landowners in the locality from some time in the 16th century until the house was sold to Pembrokeshire County Council in 1972. The east window over the altar, by Mary Lowndes of London, was installed in memory of Major John Higgon who was killed in action in 1916. It is interesting since as well as belonging to the Pembrokeshire Yeomanry, Higgon was attached to the Anzac Infantry who are portrayed in their uniforms in the background.

Returning to the porch, a much earlier memorial of 5th or 6th-century date has been moved here from the churchyard. The Latin script is generally accepted as: 'EVALI FILI DENCUI CUNIOVENDE MATER EIUS' – '[The stone of] Evalus son of Dencuus; Cuniovende his mother [set it up].'

Looking down into the churchyard from the porch, a tree stump shows where, in 1988, storm damage took down part of an ash tree. The remainder of the tree had to be removed. The staves of the church wardens were fashioned from the timber by James Harries, the woodturner in Mathry. In 1988, a study of the churchyard flora identified 60 species, emphasising how low-maintenance church-yards are a haven for wild species of flowering plants and trees.

From the church in Spittal, proceed west for 0.5ml to Spittal Cross to join a narrow road north (right) towards Little Newcastle. After 2.3ml, take the left-hand fork and continue north for a further 1.8ml to Little Newcastle. On the way the pilgrim passes a farm called Rinaston, where the remains of a medieval chapel are still visible. Near Parc-y-Llyn nursing home and close to the edge of a field at Colston farm on the approach to Little Newcastle are two Neolithic burial chambers.

Although deemed a 'mean village' by Richard Fenton in 1811, Little Newcastle boasted three cattle and stock fairs during the year: they were Ffair Farc (St Mark's Fair), Ffair Bedr (St Peter's Fair) and a third, probably called Ffair Fach (The Little Fair). These continued into the 20th century.

The church is built on the south side of the village green on which stood an early medieval motte. Originally dedicated to St David, the church was granted as a benefice to Pill Priory by Adam de la Rupe in the 12th century. The octagonal font belongs to this period. At that time, it most probably consisted of a nave, chancel and north aisle, which appears to have been blocked off later and allowed to decay, although it was partially re-opened in 1807. In 1835, however, the Revd Peter Davies Richardson was appointed to

St Peter's, Little Newcastle

the parish, and despite a lack of funds and the general poverty of the parish, he decided that if the drift away to the chapels was to be halted something had to be done about the state of his church. Several plans were considered by the Church Incorporated Building Society for an enlargement of the building. A desperate correspondence between the Society and the vicar continued until 1845. Despite the intervention of a local landowner, the Revd Thomas Martin, on behalf of the church, no grant was received from the Society. However, the work went ahead and a larger seating capacity was provided for 148 people. But this restoration proved inadequate and by 1876 the dilapidated state of the north aisle necessitated its removal, to be replaced by a vestry and a porch giving access to the widened nave and chancel. This building has remained to the present day.

Inside, the church is beautifully maintained. In 2002, the vicar's warden is the great-great-granddaughter of the church warden who was signatory to the completion of the Revd Richardson's refurbishments. The most important recent installations have been the windows, all designed by students and lecturers in the department of stained glass at the Swansea Institute. The east window over the altar was created in the 1960s by Roy Lewis and shows Christ giving the keys of the Kingdom to St Peter. Unusually, Jesus is shown clean shaven with short hair, dressed in a scarlet robe over a white undergarment. The five windows in the nave depict, on the north side: the Birth and Baptism of Christ; and on the south: the Crucifixion, the Resurrection and the Ascension. These are the work of Caroline Loveys and were installed in the 1990s. In 2001, the west window, by John Edwards, was put in place. It portrays the Second Coming – an image of the Messiah in Glory, dressed in white. These windows form a major 20th-century contribution to the history of the church.

West window,
Little Newcastle

A study conducted between 1986 and 2000 found 96 plant species in and around the churchyard. A number of graves commemorate people who took part in national and local events.

The memorial to the most notorious native of the village is to be found on the north side of the village green. Here a large stone carries a metal plaque with the inscription:

Cas Newydd Bach	Little Newcastle
Yn y pentref yma y ganed	in this village was born
Barti Ddu	Black Barty
y môr-leidr enwog	the famous pirate
1682–1722	1682–1722

A mariner, Barty (born John Roberts) was captured by pirates who at that time plundered the seas between Africa and the Caribbean. Reluctantly, he joined them and became perhaps the most successful pirate of all time until hunted down and finally killed in an attack by Royal Navy Captain Ogle of the *Swallow* on 10 February 1722.

Besides Neolithic, Bronze and Iron Age monuments and settlements, a number of holy wells are located around the village. Two of these – Ffynnon Isa and Ucha – are at the two farms named New Ffynnonau and Ffynone to the south of the village. A third, called Ffynnon Olden, said to be a tidal well, lies about 0.3ml outside the village on the road towards Letterston.

To visit St Dogwell's church from Little Newcastle, retrace the route south across the river Anghof. For walkers, a bridlepath on the right, just over the bridge, leads on to St Dogwell's church. This was the walk, about 1ml in length, taken every Sunday by the Revd Richardson and his parishioners while St Peter's was being refurbished. The route takes the pilgrim through fields and down into the river valley past the old rectory. A little further up the hill after the bridge over the Anghof, another muddier footpath takes the walking pilgrim past New Ffynnonau and Ffynone farms and their holy wells up to Garn Turne rocks. Car travellers will continue over the Anghof for 2.3ml, turning right at the first crossroads towards the rocky mass of Garn Turne.

Cantref stone

Before exploring the rocks, it is worth stopping to look at the Cantref stone. It stands in the right-hand roadside hedge, 90 yards to the west of the farm track to Ffynone and marks the boundary of the three hundreds: Dewisland, Cemais and Daugleddau. A little further on, a wicket gate opens onto moorland surrounding Garn Turne rocks. Here lie the collapsed remains of a large burial chamber whose enormous capstone has fallen onto the side uprights. The V-shaped forecourt, like that at Pentre Ifan, is constructed of tall uprights, diminishing in size away from the chamber. In the Middle Ages, relics of St David were brought to this point, from where a view of much of all three cantrefs, now deaneries, may be obtained. It is said that the relics were brought here on 1 March each year and that the bishop and the Lords of Cemais and Daugleddau met at this spot to decide questions of mutual jurisdiction. It was one of the duties of certain tenants to escort the relics of the saint around the diocese in peacetime and in time of war. Amongst those who were expected to serve as escort to Garn Turne were tenants of Pointz Castle, Castle Morris, Trefin and Wolf's Castle, the ruling being that they should be able to return home the same night. Sometimes, the bishop directed that relics be taken to other dioceses – to north Wales in 1287, to Gloucester in

Garn Turne
burial chamber

1358 and even to Ireland in 1259. Usually, the purpose was to raise money for the diocese, and potential donors were often induced to be generous by the offer of 'indulgences' or pardons for past sins.

ST DOGWELL'S CHURCH (ST DOGFAEL)   OS SM 969 280

Less than 1ml west of Garn Turne rocks, the church of St Dogwell's, or Llantydewi as it was known in medieval times, stands in a tree-ringed glade above the rocky falls of the Anghof river which joins the Cleddau at Wolf's Castle. Richard Fenton records a village in the fields opposite the church but, though the ground is uneven, no surface traces remain. In 1254, the benefice was appropriated to the chapter of St Davids Cathedral. The nave and chancel, with a bellcote on the west end, are separated from a south aisle by low arches whose capitals are

St Dogwell's church

decorated with a twisted cord pattern and animal-headed motifs similar to those at Llawhaden. At the east end of the south aisle, a mortuary chapel was established in 1328 by Sir Richard Symond of Sealyham in return for the services of two priests who were required to say Masses for his soul and that of Eleanor his wife.

The church was restored in 1872 and tiles were laid to cover memorials on the floor. At the same time, the body of a tiny child was found buried in the west wall with a little cross and green stone amulet. Memorials in the south aisle and the stained glass windows commemorate members of the Tucker Edwards family from Sealyham, across the lane from the church. The Tuckers were first recorded at Treffgarne early in the 15th century and by the middle of the 16th century owned Sealyham estate. In the 18th century, Admiral Thomas Tucker supposedly killed the pirate Blackbeard in the West Indies – an interesting fact in view of the origins of the notorious Bartholomew Roberts in nearby Little Newcastle. Tucker's great-niece married an Edwards, taking on both names. It was here that Captain John Tucker Edwards in the 19th century bred the famous Sealyham terriers. After the death of his nephew in 1902, the estate fell into debt and in 1920 the house was sold to the King Edward VII National Memorial Association, becoming a hospital for tuberculosis sufferers. Since 1988 it has been an Activity Centre popular with educational and youth groups and holiday makers.

In 1814, Joseph Harris (1773–1825) – author, editor and hymn writer, who was married in this church – launched the first weekly newspaper in Welsh, *Seren Gomer*. Despite efforts to keep it going, the newspaper failed after 85 issues and Harris had to sell, but J. D. Lewis, who established himself as a printer in Llandysul in 1892, held Harris in such admiration that he named his business 'The Gomerian Press'. Now called Gomer Press, the business exists to this day.

The stone which stands on the west side of the churchyard recalls an older period of parish history. The inscription in Latin script reads 'HOGTIVIS FILI DEMETI' – 'Hogtivis, son of Demetus'. The stone was originally used as a gatepost at Little Treffgarne to the south, reputedly the birthplace of Owain Glyndŵr. According to legend, Glyndŵr lies buried behind Allt-yr-Afon in Wolf's Castle. A photograph exists of another cross stone, attached to a pigsty in Wolf's Castle village, but this has disappeared.

Hogtivis stone

From St Dogwell's, the road descends to the bridge over the river and up past the entrance to Sealyham. A left turn just beyond the drive takes the pilgrim to a crossroads on the A40. Here it is advisable to follow an OS map. Hayscastle Cross is reached either by continuing straight on through Welsh Hook or by turning south into Wolf's Castle and right at the Wolfe Inn. At the Cross Inn at Hayscastle the road continues west for 0.3ml to a crossroads near Hayscastle Tump. A left turn here will lead the pilgrim towards Roch and to the next church on the trail, Brawdy.

Roch Castle

From Hayscastle Cross, the pilgrim joins the A487 at Roch, the site of a 13th-century castle whose remaining D-shaped tower, dominating the surrounding landscape, is built on an igneous rocky outcrop. The road west runs parallel to the beach at Newgale Sands. At Penycwm, turn right inland and proceed for about 1ml, skirting disused Brawdy Airfield, before turning right, down a farm lane towards the church.

Many medieval pilgrims chose to land at the beach at Newgale in order to avoid the treacherous tides in Ramsey Sound, and religious talismans and tokens including necklaces from European and Near Eastern shrines have been discovered there. 1ml inland along quiet lanes, the small double-bellcote church stands near Brawdy farm, which in the Middle Ages was a manor house belonging to the bishops of St Davids. The raised circular churchyard, which is full of extravagant Victorian memorials, suggests a pre-Norman foundation, and Brawdy may have been the site of a Dark Age Christian burial-ground. The name Brawdy – probably an anglicised form of the Welsh 'Breudeth' – suggests that the original church was dedicated not to St David but to the Irish saint, Brigid. Other explanations of the name Brawdy have also been offered: 'The House of Judgement' ('Brawd-dŷ'), pointing to the court or seat of judgement of a Welsh prince, and 'The House of the Brethren', which would indicate the

St David's, Brawdy

Brawdy, interior

presence of a hospice in the locality, at which monks would offer food and shelter to pilgrims travelling west to the shrine of St David.

The nave and chancel are probably 13th century; restoration work was carried out in 1879 and 1901. Still visible are the corbels on which the rood-loft once rested and the remains of steps leading up to the loft. A pointed arch separates the nave from the south transept or aisle which, together with the Rice family chapel to the south of the chancel, represent a 15th-century modification of an early squinch arch. The peculiar gap in the south wall of the nave is probably the original pre-15th-century window. The 'weeping' chancel inclines north, and it has been suggested that the nave is aligned to the St Brigid's Day sunrise on 1 February and the chancel to the St David's Day sunrise on 1 March. The font (on a modern base) is Norman, and according to local legend, the dents in it were made by Cromwell's soldiers who used it to sharpen their swords in the belief that this would make them invulnerable. The bell at the west end is dated 1639.

The church houses four 5th–6th-century Christian inscribed stones. Three, gathered from around the parish, are located in the porch. One, which was once used as part of a footbridge on Caswilia or Castle Villa farm to the north, has a Latin and Ogham dedication to 'Vendognus' and the other a Latin and Ogham inscription recording 'the son of Quagte'. A third stone, which used to serve as a gatepost at Rickeston Hall, bears the name 'Briacus'. The fourth stone, which was discovered in the yard of Brawdy farm, is on the left as one enters the nave and is dedicated to 'Maccutrenus, son of Catomaglus'.

LLANDELOY CHURCH (ST TEILO)   OS SM 857 267

From Brawdy church, continue north, passing Trefgarn Owen. Turn left at the next junction and left again at the next crossroads. The church is located on the left on the way out of the village of Llandeloy, 0.6ml further along this road.

The dedication to St Teilo is a mistake that can be traced back to the early 18th century. Little can be said definitively as to the original dedication – both Eloi and Tylwyf have been suggested as founding saints, but both are conjectural. As photographs in the church attest, the church lay in a ruinous state from 1840 to 1925, having been used previously as a school. In 1924, however, the parish and the Church Incorporated Building Society raised the money to reconstruct the church from fragmentary 12th-century remains.

The architect was John Coates Carter (1859–1927), and Llandeloy, considered to be his masterpiece, represents a unique example of a medieval church sympathetically restored in the spirit of the pre-

St Teilo's, Llandeloy

Llandeloy, interior

Conquest foundation but at the same time creatively reinvented by the Arts and Crafts movement. Building work began in 1925 and was completed in the summer of the following year. Coates Carter's dynamic vision succeeded in creating far more than a mere 'replica' of a Welsh medieval structure. Situated on a gentle slope, the bellcote church, with its long, unbroken roofline, has a primitive, barn-like appearance. Its north-east end seems to burrow into the hillside. Inside, one is immediately impressed by a sense of dense solidity and by the striking contrast between the stone walls and the wooden joinery. As Phil Thomas has noted, 'it has something of the intense, sheltering stillness and mystery of a cave or rock-cut shrine'. Dominating the interior is the rood-screen and loft, made from English oak, which separate the weeping chancel from the nave. For the modern pilgrim used to post-Reformation architecture, such lofts and screens may seem strangely unfamiliar, but they were once a feature of numerous Pembrokeshire churches. A pulpit, also made of oak, is located against the screen on

94

the north side, and access to both loft and pulpit is gained via the rood-stair on the same side. To the south, a transeptal chapel opens into the nave though a medieval arch and into the chancel through a squinch. The medieval octagonal font at the west end is set on a series of steep steps. Thomas has rightly described Coates Carter's superb (re)creation as 'the last incandescence of a magnificent Welsh tradition'.

To the south of the church among undergrowth, a freshwater spring bubbles up into a stone-ringed well which used to supply the village with water.

Just over 1ml north of the church at Treffynnon is a damaged 4th–early 3rd millennium BC chambered tomb consisting of a fallen capstone resting on one of three uprights (OS SM 854 286). Permission to visit the site must be sought at the farm.

Holy well, Llandeloy

Llanhywel/ Llanhowel Church (St Hywel)   OS SM 818 274

Take the left turning at the crossroads north of Llandeloy and continue west for 2.4ml to Llanhywel.

The tiny gem of a church stands in a slightly raised churchyard, awash with flowers in spring, on a site occupied in the 6th century by a religious settlement that may have been part of the monastic community or *clas* based at St Davids. It is a place of great tranquillity. The founding of the present Norman church probably dates from the episcopacy of Bishop Bernard of St Davids (1115–48). The nave and chancel are 12th–early 13th century while the vaulted north chapel is a late 13th–early 14th-century addition. The lead in the window of the chapel is 15th century, and in the west wall is a blocked-up leper's squint which afforded a view of the altar. Corbels, originally

St Hywel badge
(Croesgoch C.P. School)

St Hywel or Hoel (6th century)

Feast Day: 31 October

Hywel, known also as Hywel Farchog ('The Knight') and St Hoel, was another of the sons of Emyr Llydaw and was forced to flee Armorica (Brittany) because of internecine strife. He figures in the Welsh medieval tales of the *Mabinogion* as a knight of King Arthur's court and as one of the king's counsellors. The Welsh Triads refer to him as one of the three 'Royal Knights' of the court, famed for his courage, prowess in battle and courtesy. On a modern painted panel in Llanhywel church is a representation of St Hywel in the company of King Aercol Lawhir of Dyfed and Bishop Teilo. He is supposed to be buried at Llanilltud Fawr. Geoffrey of Monmouth's *History of the Kings of Britain* (c. 1136) transforms him into King Hoel the Great of Brittany, who came to aid his relation Arthur and who 'in Arthur's company conquered many countries'.

St Hywel's, Llanhywel

supporting a rood-loft, are visible on the chancel arch. The cushion font is 12th century. Restored in the 1870s, the church has preserved its medieval simplicity and character.

Set into a cement plinth at the west end is a 6th-century Christian inscribed gravemarker or memorial stone. As is the case with so many Pembrokeshire pillar-stones, this once served as a farm gatepost – in this instance at Upper Carnhedryn. In the 1890s it was bought by one Henry Owen for £5 and placed in the porch of the church of St James the Great at Carnhedryn (now a private dwelling). It bears the inscription 'RINACI NOMENA' – either 'The name of Rinacus' or, more probably, 'Rinacus the Martyr'.

The aumbry in the passage leading from the north chapel to the chancel is covered by a painted panel by Marguerite Hawkett entitled 'The Donation', commemorating two members of the Pringle family killed in the First and Second World Wars. It depicts a seated St Teilo as Bishop with King Aercol Lawhir (a 6th-century ruler of Dyfed) kneeling in front of him. The figure behind the king is St Hywel, also known

Llanhywel, interior
(*photo:* Edward Perkins)

97

as St Hoel, the patron of the church and a disciple of Teilo. Tradition holds that Aercol enlisted the help of the bishop to bring his wayward royal household into line, in exchange for which Teilo was granted land. Teilo presented some of this land to Hywel on which to found a church.

From Llanhywel, the pilgrim's route leads south to the hamlet of Middle Mill. Before continuing the journey, however, the pilgrim may choose to visit sites of interest around Llanhywel.

The road leading north from Llanhywel to the main A487 passes the prominent rocky outcrop of Carn Treglemais in a field on the left, which commands views over St Davids peninsula. Bearing right at the fork, the road passes through Treglemais farm. In summer, the air above the whitewashed buildings is thronged with swifts and martins. Treglemais, known in ecclesiastical records as Villa Clementi and Clemenston – 'Clement's Estate' – was an episcopal manor, granted in 1332 to the Bishop of St Davids, Henry de Gower.

Neolithic and Bronze Age ritual has also left its mark on the landscape around Llanhywel. 0.7ml north-east of the church in a large field on Tresewig farm (permission must be sought) is an imposing 4th–early 3rd millennium BC burial chamber known as the White Horse, consisting of five stocky uprights and a massive capstone (OS SM 825 284). The nonconformist denominations have also built impressively here: at Caerfarchell, to the west of Llanhywel, is a fine Calvinistic Methodist chapel dating from 1827 (OS SM 795 270).

Middle Mill, Whitchurch, St Elvis and Nine Wells

From Llanhywel, walkers should take the bridleway south of the church and cross the river Solva at Caerforiog Bridge. Motorists, however, should proceed north from Llanhywel for just under 1ml (bearing left at the fork) to join the main A487 south. After a further 1ml, turn left at Carnhedryn and proceed for 0.8ml to Caerforiog Bridge.

Caerforiog farm, a short distance beyond the bridge, was the site of an ancient homestead where Adam de Houghton, Bishop of St Davids from 1361 to 1389, is said to have been born. To the north of the present buildings is a moat, and a dovecot stood close by. The complex also comprised a chapel, parts of which were still visible as late as 1925. Two fine megaliths of the 2nd millennium BC are located at Tremaenhir farm ('Farm of the Standing Stone'), 1ml east (OS SM 827 263).

Continuing south from Caerforiog, a right turn after 0.2ml takes the pilgrim westwards to rejoin the river at Middle

St Elvis/ Elfyw/ Aelfyw/ Ailbe
(d. between 526 and 541)
Feast Day: 12 September

St Elvis, the name of the farm lying on the coast near Solva, 4ml east of St Davids, is an anglicisation of the Welsh Llaneilw or Llanelfyw – 'the church of [Saint] Elfyw'. Elfyw, or Ailbe, to give him his Irish name, was Bishop of Emly in Munster and is a figure around whom many legends have accrued. Irish sources tell how he was abandoned in the forest and suckled by a she-wolf. Years later, the saint repaid the favour by saving the grizzled beast from the huntsman. Other sources identify him as a confessor at St Davids. In Welsh genealogies, he figures as the cousin of St David, whom he is supposed to have baptised at the ancient harbour of Porth Clais, south of St Davids. A holy spring, subsequently known as Ffynnon Ddewi, is said to have flowed at the moment of baptism. There was a medieval chapel on the site, and Browne Willis in 1715 records that the water of the holy spring was collected in a cistern under the east gable of the building. The well was last seen in 1950.

Mill. Today, visitors are drawn to the hamlet's woollen mill, which has been in production since 1907. There was a mill here in medieval times belonging to the Bishop of St Davids, as well as an *ysbyty* or hospice: a ridge of land to the south bears the name Clyn-ysbyty – 'the spur of land by the hospice'. 0.3ml west is the 13th-century church of St David at Whitchurch. In Welsh, Whitchurch parish is known as Plwy'r Groes and the hamlet near the church as Tregroes – a reference to the ancient village cross near the churchyard gate, of which only the stump survives, known as Maen Dewi (not to be confused with the megalith of the same name on Dowrog Common), at which pilgrims used to rest before entering St Davids. 0.6ml south of Middle Mill the road joins the main A487 at the village of Solva (possibly from the Norse for 'sunny ford') with its once busy natural harbour and lime kilns under the headland known as the Gribin.

Burial chamber, St Elvis farm

1ml east, 400m south of St Elvis farm, is a large, possibly double-chambered, 4th–early 3rd millennium BC tomb (OS SM 812 239). It is known that in the 18th and 19th centuries, parts of the tomb were blasted and removed by the tenant farmers. The location of the farm itself is also of interest: this was the site of St Teilo's church, which was still visible in the early 1940s. Numerous early Christian graves were discovered here. The ancient font from the church, together with a cross-inscribed stone known as Maen Dewi – yet another stone bearing this name – are now kept in St Aidan's church in Solva.

Travelling west towards St David, one passes through the hamlet of Nine Wells (a name testifying to the numerous natural springs in the area) and enters Cylch Dewi – the sacred landscape of St David.

Cylch Dewi –
The Sacred Landscape of St David

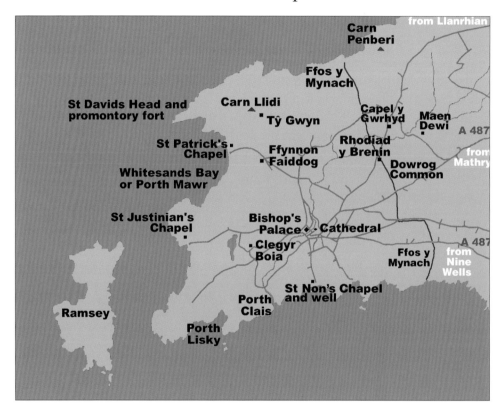

Carn Penberi

from Llanrhian

Ffos y Mynach

St Davids Head and promontory fort

Carn Llidi

Tŷ Gwyn

Capel y Gwrhyd

Maen Dewi

A 487

St Patrick's Chapel

Ffynnon Faiddog

Rhodiad y Brenin

from Mathry

Whitesands Bay or Porth Mawr

Dowrog Common

St Justinian's Chapel

Bishop's Palace

Cathedral

A 487

Clegyr Boia

Ffos y Mynach

from Nine Wells

Ramsey

Porth Clais

St Non's Chapel and well

Porth Lisky

CYLCH DEWI –
THE SACRED LANDSCAPE OF ST DAVID

As the pilgrim crosses Ffos y Mynach – 'The Monk's Dyke', marking the old boundary of Menevia – at Capel y Gwrhyd from the north, reaches St Non's from the south or east, or arrives by sea at Whitesands Bay, St Justinian's or the harbour of Porth Clais, he or she enters a sacred landscape, encircled by the shrines, chapels and ancient burial grounds which are integral to the medieval ecclesiastical topography of the place. Pilgrims arriving by land or sea at the chapels on the peninsula around St Davids would leave offerings at these smaller shrines. The offerings were made out of devotion and gratitude but they were not always so received. Browne Willis, writing in 1716, describes how 'what was there offered . . . was brought on Saturdays to the Chapter house and there divided by dishfulls, the quantity not allowing them to tell it' – not between the various needs of the Cathedral, whose fabric was in grave need of repair, but between the canons and priests.

St David badge
(St Davids V.A. School)

St David or Dewi Sant (d. 589)

Feast Day: 1 March

St David, reputedly conceived out of wedlock, was of noble birth. His mother was St Non and his father, Sant, was ruler of Ceredigion. Some time previously, Sant had deposited at a monastery the three omens which were to foreshadow the life of David: a honeycomb for wisdom, a stag for power and a fish for abstinence. He is supposed to have been born at St Non's near St Davids, where the impress of Non's hands in labour left their mark on the stone to which she clung. David's miracles began at the moment of his baptism at Porth Clais, when the sight of the blind and aged Movi was restored. He also opened the blind eyes of his teacher Paulinus with whom he is said to have studied at Henfynw – Old Menevia – south of Aberaeron in Ceredigion. Having founded a number of religious houses in the West Country and the Welsh Marches, he came with his disciples to the Vallis Rosina – the valley of the little marsh – where the Cathedral now stands. His monastic institution was initially threatened by opposition from the local Irish chieftain Boia and his wife, but David negotiated these early difficulties and kings and princes flocked to his foundation. The monastic rule adopted was one of work, prayer and ascetic living, in imitation of the monks and desert hermits of Egypt. Under the direction of an angel, he journeyed with St Teilo and St Padarn to Jerusalem, where the patriarch consecrated David archbishop and presented the three holy men with gifts: a bell, a staff, an altar and a tunic woven with gold. On his return, David was persuaded, reluctantly, to preach against the heresy of Pelagius at a synod called to Llanddewi Brefi to elect an archbishop for the British race. On his way, he restored to life the dead child of a widow. At the synod, the mound of garments on which he preached became a high hill so that he could be heard by all, and a white dove settled on his shoulder. Years later, summoned by angels with the news that St David's death was imminent, crowds flocked to St Davids and on 1 March, after he had blessed them and enjoined them to follow his teaching, he died. The air was filled with a sweet fragrance and the songs of angels.

Capel y Gwrhyd (Chapel of the Fathom)   OS SM 768 275

The coast road from Llanrhian continues south through Berea, Waun Beddau ('Field of the Graves'), past the farmsteads of Gwrhyd Mawr and Gwrhyd Bach and into Rhodiad y Brenin. This is a place of numerous springs and wells, and can be considered the gateway to the sacred landscape of St David. A field near the road is called Parc y Capel, marking the site of an important medieval chapel. It was marked on Ogilby's 1675 map, but no trace of it survives. 'Gwrhyd' means 'the span of a man's arms' and is the Welsh for 'fathom' – 6 feet or 2 metres. The name of the chapel seems to derive from a representation of the saint with outstretched arms (perhaps originally a depiction of the crucifixion) which Browne Willis described in the early 18th century as 'St David's Fathom upon an arch of the chapel'. The holy water stoup from Capel y Gwrhyd is now housed in the modern Chapel of Our Lady and St Non overlooking St Non's Bay, south of St Davids. Preserved in the name Rhodiad y Brenin – 'The King's Walk' – is a reference to Henry II, who passed through here in September 1171 on a pilgrimage to St Davids Cathedral, on his way to Ireland to ensure that the power of the Norman baron Richard de Clare ('Strongbow') remained in check. *Brut y Tywysogion – The Chronicle of the Princes* – records that Henry presented the Cathedral with two copes of brocaded silk and a handful of silver. He also dined with Bishop David FitzGerald. On his return from Ireland in April of the following year, he paid a second visit to the Cathedral, landing at St Justinian's and proceeding to the Cathedral in pilgrim's garb to hear Mass. Henry was following in the footsteps of another royal pilgrim – William the Conqueror – who had visited the Cathedral a century earlier.

Modern pilgrims entering St Davids either on the coast road from Llanrhian or on the main A487 skirt the marshy area of some 200 acres known as Dowrog Common (from the Welsh 'dyfr(i)og', meaning 'watery'). Managed by the Wildlife Trust, West Wales, it sustains rare flora and fauna and has been designated a Site of Special Scientific Interest. Fourteen different species of dragonfly have been found here. The area was known in Welsh as Tir Pererinion ('Pilgrims' Land'), and was a gift to the Church from Rhys ap Tewdwr, King of Deheubarth (south Wales), in 1091. Behind a

house called Drws Gobaith ('The Doorway of Hope') on the northern fringe of the common is an impressive megalith, 8 feet in height, known as Maen Dewi ('David's Stone'); it dates from the 2nd millennium BC (OS SM 775 275). In the early 1800s, the stone was incorporated into the wall of a *tŷ unnos* – a 'one-night' or 'moonlight' house – which lies ruined next to the stone. According to ancient rights of tenure, an individual who built a house on common land in a single night and had smoke issuing from the chimney by morning was entitled to the house and a portion of the land surrounding it, which

Butterfly orchid, Dowrog Common

could then be farmed. The practical builder of this particular *tŷ unnos* saved a good deal of time by utilising the huge stone as a substantial part of one of his walls.

St Patrick's Chapel, Whitesands Bay   OS SM 734 272

From Llanrhian on the coast road, a turning to the right just before one enters the city of St Davids is signposted to Whitesands beach. There is a fee at the car park during holiday months. Opposite the car park, a gate to the right of the road leads onto the Coast Path and almost immediately to St Patrick's chapel.

Only the foundations of the trapezoid-shaped chapel, traditionally attributed to St Patrick, remain and a plaque shows the position of the altar prior to excavations on the site in 1924. These uncovered a building, some 33 feet long overall and tapering towards the west,

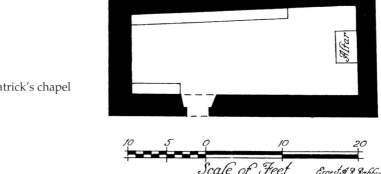

Plan of St Patrick's chapel

Whitesands Bay viewed from St Patrick's chapel

with walls of unmortared rough stone and infill of sandy clay. At the east end, a stone altar was asymmetrically placed towards the north wall; near the doorway a heap of stones indicated an original arch or wall, and ledges along the south and north walls may have provided seating. As well as the remains of a piscina or holy water stoup, several burials were found: two complete male skeletons – one a young man aligned east–west near the altar – and three skulls – two complete, the third in fragments. Associated with the burials were pieces of white quartz and quantities of limpet shells. In 1856, the chapel was described as being in the middle of a field – indeed, the field to the east is still known locally as Parc y Capel – but the sea has since encroached on the site. A climb down the eroded low cliff of windblown sand and boulder clay on which the chapel was built reveals a number of levels of white quartz blocks separated by sand and clay. The association of white stones and mollusc shells with small shrines is relatively frequent and their stratigraphic sequence here may indicate successive phases of chapel building.

The association with St Patrick derives from traditional accounts of the saint's desire to settle in this place. In Rhygyfarch's 11th-century *Life of St David*, it is St Patrick who first seeks to set up his church at Menevia; warned by an angel that it was reserved for another, however, he sailed west to begin his mission in Ireland. Tŷ Gwyn, on the slopes of Carn Llidi nearby, may have been the site of the Monastery of the Deposit to which Sant, father of David, is said to have entrusted the three gifts (a honeycomb, a stag and a fish) which foreshadowed the life of his son.

There is also a tradition that St David built his first church, Yr Hen Eglwys, beneath the sands of the burrows on the south side of the road to the beach opposite Ffynnon Faiddog. John Leland, writing for Henry VIII in the 16th century, thought this exposed promontory was the site of Roman *Menapia*, but there has been no archaeological evidence to support the idea, apart from a few coins. However, there are Neolithic burial chambers on the upper slopes of Carn Llidi and on St Davids Head, at the end of which is a fine Iron Age fort defended by flower-strewn sea cliffs to the north and south and by triple stone ramparts to the east. Within it are the foundations of six houses. Below, between the headland and Carn Llidi, is an ancient field system; it may still be partially seen in winter.

St Justinian,
Stinan or Iestyn
(6th century)
Feast Day:
5 December

St Justinian badge
(Tredafydd V.C. School)

The son of a Breton prince, Justinian left home to follow the teaching of Christ. On Ramsey Island, he was invited to join the hermit cell or *clas* established there by Honorius and his sister. He agreed, on condition that all women withdrew from the island. His rule was strict and devout and much admired by St David, who made him his confessor and granted him lands near Lower Treginnis, a farm on St Davids peninsula, for the maintenance of his island community. In protest against the ascetic rule, his disciples faked a message claiming St David was ill and needed him. As they rowed him across, Justinian sensed evil and turned to see his followers changed to devils flying off in the shape of crows, leaving him to brave the waves on his stone altar. Finally, on 25 August 537, in total revolt, his servants cut off his head; where it fell, a pure spring of water welled up. Justinian promptly snatched up his head and crossed treacherous Ramsey Sound before collapsing on the site of his chapel. His murderers were condemned as lepers to live out their lives mid-channel on Leper's Rock.

St Justinian's Chapel
OS SM 723 253

The chapel is well signposted out of St Davids. The journey can also be made on foot along the Coast Path from Whitesands Bay.

The shell of the chapel dedicated to St Justinian lies about 1.75ml west of the Cathedral, alongside the Coast Path and the flight of steps leading down to Porthstinian and the lifeboat station – the embarkation point for trips to Ramsey and the islands.

As the network of lanes around St Davids emerges onto the peninsula, the mass of Clegyr Boia can be seen on the left. Excavation has shown that this was a Neolithic settlement followed by an Iron Age stronghold. It also features in the *Life of St David* as the settlement of Boia and his wife who threatened and abused the saint and his monks continually. The *Life* tells of the couple's temporary repentance when their cattle were struck dead in response to an assault on David; of the wife and her maids playing lascivious games in full view of the saint and his monks while they were at prayer; of the wife killing her own stepdaughter and falling into madness; and of how Boia's fortress was destroyed by fire sent from heaven.

Above the little bay of Porthstinian, the chapel marks the place where, according to accounts of his life, St Justinian collapsed after crossing Ramsey Sound. It was here that his body was first buried, until removed, it was claimed, by St David to the site of his own tomb in the Vallis Rosina.

Ruins of St Justinian's chapel, showing remains of the tower

The first mention of a chapel on the site is by John of Tynemouth about 1350. The present building dates to the episcopate of Edward Vaughan (1506–23). By the time of the earliest descriptions, it was already partially in ruins. A description by Browne Willis in 1716 records 'a very fine strong building . . . with battlements round it and a tower at one end, in which there were bells formerly. The walls are still very strong, tho' there has been no covering upon it these many years.' There was also a well by the chapel. Jones and Freeman, writing nearly a century and a half later in 1856, are more detailed in their description of the architecture, which they call 'plain perpendicular'; the dimensions they noted were 40 feet x 17 feet 6 inches, with walls 12 feet in height. The parapets mentioned by Browne Willis had disappeared by this time. They also remark on the internal arches and the traces of a piscina pecked out of a stone block and draw an analogy with the church of St Fiacre, Penmarch, Brittany to emphasise that the tower also served as a lighthouse – appropriately, of course, for a chapel mainly used for the devotions of mariners. From cliffs above the lifeboat station, Ramsey Island, where St Justinian and others set up their religious community, seems very close, but the tide race between reaches 8 knots, and the spikes of the Bitches, the Horse and Gwahan Garreg ('leper's rock') on which Justinian's murderers were forced to end their days render the passage interesting on a fine day and hazardous in storms.

Dedications to St Justinian are not common. There are three in Pembrokeshire: this chapel, the church at Llanstinan, and in a similar situation close to a stream in a sheltered valley, the parish church of Lower Freystrop, south of Haverfordwest.

St Non's Well and Chapel
(OS SM 751 243)

Pilgrims may choose to walk to St Non's from St Justinian's on the Coast Path, or drive back into St Davids, from where St Non's is signposted. From Nine Wells, travel into St Davids, bearing left at the 14th-century preaching cross in the centre of the city, down Goat Street. Keep bearing left round the corner and take the road immediately left signposted to St Non's (0.3ml). There is ample parking on the clifftop.

St Non's Well, which gives access to the chapel in the field below, was described by Browne Willis in the early 18th century as 'a fine Well . . . covered with a stone roof, and enclosed within a wall, with benches to sit upon . . . Some old simple people go still to visit this saint at some particular times, especially on St Non's Day (March 2) which they keep holy and offer pins, pebbles etc.' The cowl over the present well was restored in the 18th century and in 1951 by the Roman Catholic Church; the earlier 'stone roof' described by Browne Willis

St Non (5th–6th century)

Feast Day: 2 or 3 March

Non (also known as Nun, Nonna and Nonnita and called Non Fendigaid or 'The Blessed') may have been of noble birth, the daughter of Cynyr and Anna. Rhygyfarch's *Life of St David* (compiled *c.* 1094) claims she was a member of a religious community in the vicinity of St Davids and was violated by Sant, King of Ceredigion. The birth of David, traditionally held to have taken place on the site marked by ruined St Non's Chapel, was accompanied by apocalyptic weather. After the death of Sant, Non became a nun and journeyed to Altarnon in Cornwall, where a church and well are dedicated to her. In Wales, there are dedications to her in Cardiganshire and Carmarthenshire. She is also venerated in Brittany, where she is always portrayed holding an open book. Her impressive tomb can be seen at Dirinon near Brest in Finistère, and a Breton mystery play, *Buez Santes Nonn*, was performed at Dirinon during the later Middle Ages.

St Non's Well

would have been similar, though the well complex would have been a good deal larger. The holy spring reputedly flowed from the earth at the birth of St David; indeed, the water was at one time used in the Cathedral. As Browne Willis's account testifies, St Non's was used as a healing well – particularly efficacious, it seems, in the treatment of eye complaints and rheumatism – long after the Reformation. The historian and topographer Richard Fenton records that as an infant he was 'often dipped' into the well, which 'shone with votive brass'.

Dramatically located near the Coast Path on a south-facing slope above St Non's Bay with the expanse of St Bride's Bay beyond, the ruined chapel of St Non looks out over Skomer Island. On a clear day, one can catch a glimpse of Grassholm. Tradition holds that St Non gave birth to St David on this spot during a great storm in the 6th century. A Bronze Age stone half-circle surrounds the site. As seen today, the simple building, one of the most important pilgrimage chapels around St Davids, probably dates from the early 14th century, but the foundation is much older – perhaps as early as the 8th century. 'Stone coffins' were discovered here in the early 19th century which may have been early Christian graves. The chapel is unusually aligned north–south: this may be the result of architectural improvisation on the sloping ground, but it is also possible that the chapel is only a single transept of a much larger building. The thickness of the masonry at the north-west corner of the chapel seems to reinforce this. Resting against the south-west corner of the chapel is a 7th–9th-century stone, incised with a linear ring-cross. Although it was once built into the chapel's walls, it is not known whether the pillar-stone was originally associated with this site. The chapel fell out of use at the Reformation and was used as a dwelling house and subsequently as a leek garden.

To the east of the medieval chapel is the modern monastery known as St Non's Retreat House and, nearby, the Chapel of Our Lady and St Non. The latter was built in 1934, and its architecture gives a good impression of what a pilgrimage chapel on this exposed peninsula would have looked like in medieval times. Above the altar, which comprises fragments of medieval stonework, is a stained glass window depicting St Non and the young David arriving in Brittany. At the west end near the door is the holy water stoup from another important medieval chapel, Capel y Gwrhyd, near Rhodiad y Brenin north of St Davids, of which nothing now remains. At Llanon, 1ml east of Llanrhian, there used to be another medieval chapel dedicated to St Non. Reputedly part of the altar of this chapel was a stone (now lost) inscribed with Ogham markings which were traditionally said to be the impressions left by the fingers of St Non as she gave birth to St David. Ruined St Non's Chapel is also associated with the tale.

Inscribed stone, St Non's Chapel

ST DAVID'S SHRINE, ST DAVIDS CATHEDRAL

OS SM 752 254

North-west approach to St Davids Cathedral

Pilgrims have been arriving at St Davids over the centuries in the hope of gaining spiritual renewal. Though the essential nature of their journey has remained the same – something that marks the modern pilgrim to St Davids as a member of a spiritual community spanning 1,400 years – the forms and physical objects of worship have changed since the saint was reputedly buried in the grounds of his monastery. The cult of St David in the pre-Norman church was not concerned with his bodily remains but rather with his possessions in life – bell, book, staff and clothing. These were not all kept at St Davids but were retained at various shrines around the country: Llanddewi Brefi in Ceredigion, Glascwm in Powys and Llangyfelach on the Gower peninsula. At one time, some of these objects were even removed

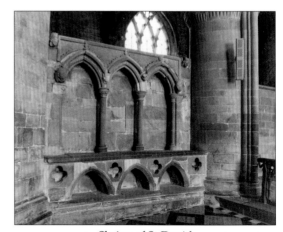

Shrine of St David

to Glastonbury: this may have been for safekeeping in response to the devastating waves of Viking raids suffered by St Davids during the 9th, 10th and 11th centuries. But the relics of the saint must also have been venerated, since Rhys ap Tewdwr and Gruffudd ap Cynan swore allegiance on them before the battle of Mynydd Carn in 1081 – the same year William the Conqueror came to St Davids as a pilgrim.

The Middle Ages saw a greater interest in recovering the body of the saint. Bernard, the first Norman bishop, searched for them in vain, but to John de Gamages, a 13th-century prior of Ewenny, its whereabouts were revealed in a dream – a discovery which gave the impetus to build the shrine in 1275. Today, this is in place between pillars on the north side of the presbytery, though its original position is not known and its appearance much changed. It is a triple-arched stone structure with apertures beneath, possibly for offerings. Early accounts describe a painted wooden coving and the arches once contained paintings or images of St David, St Patrick and St Denis, remains of which survived until the end of the 16th century. Recent thinking has suggested that the third saint in the triptych may have been St Justinian rather than St Denis. In 1089, the shrine was despoiled. The reliquary of the saint lies within a casket in a recess behind

Pilgrim token of St Thomas à Becket

117

an iron grille in the Chapel of the Holy Trinity at the back of the High Altar. The casket was the gift of the patriarchs of the Orthodox Church in 1925. It contains bones recovered from the recess during the restoration of the Cathedral by Sir Gilbert Scott – remains which are said to belong to both St Justinian and St David. Carbon-dating tests in 1995, however, established more recent dates for these remains. The new dating evidence gave rise to a suggestion that some of the bones may belong to the 11th-century saint, Caradog, but it is fairly certain that he is entombed in the shrine dedicated to him in the north transept behind the quire. A chapel dedicated to Archbishop Thomas à Becket in the north transept and a pilgrim token found locally affirm devotion to the shrine of this 12th-century saint.

While the shrines have been the objects of religious devotion and pilgrimage, a political element has also attached to them. In 1285, to mark his defeat of Llywelyn, the last native Prince of Wales, Edward I paraded the head of St David and the most sacred relics of Wales through London. Appointed in 1536 to implement the ideas of the Reformation, Bishop Barlow tried to stamp out all devotion to St David's shrine and relics. However, despite orders given in 1538 for such objects to be destroyed, he could not prevent the canons and people from 'wilfully solemnising' the saint's feast day. Much of the feeling for St David has survived as part of a strong national consciousness and political identity in Wales. Of the four patron saints of Britain, he alone belongs to the land of his birth, and though nearly 700 years have passed since Pope Callixtus authorised pilgrimage to St Davids as an alternative to Rome or Jerusalem, people come every year from all over the world to experience the beauty and spirituality of this sanctuary of clear air suspended between the boisterous seas and the solidity of the ancient land.

Appendix
Places to eat and stay on the pilgrim ways

Pilgrims from the Sea

Bridge End Inn, Llanychaer. Proprietor: A. Billington; tel: 01348 872545. Lunch, teas, evening meals. Children and muddy walkers welcome.

Ivybridge, Dyffryn, Goodwick. Proprietors: Colin and Christine Phillips; tel: 01348 875366/872623/872338. Dinner, bed and breakfast. Snacks and packed lunches prepared as required. Infants, children and dogs welcome.

Stephanie's Tea Rooms, Mathry. Proprietor: Stephanie Thomas; tel: 01348 831959. Light lunches, tea, coffee, cakes and sandwiches all day. Children welcome and dogs in the garden.

Farmer's Arms, Mathry. Proprietors: Sally and Bryan Farmer; tel: 01348 831284. Full menu for lunch 12pm–2.30pm and evening meal 6pm–9pm; snacks and bar meals also available. There is a garden room for children and well-behaved dogs are welcome.

Tregwynt Woollen Mill and shop, Aber Mawr. Proprietor: Mr Eifion Griffiths; tel: 01348 891288. Open 10am–4.30pm all year. Teas, coffees, light luncheons. Children welcome. Play area and car park.

Square and Compass Inn, Square and Compass. Proprietors: Gerald and Peggy Salmon; tel: 01348 831420. Bar meals all day and tea, coffee and sandwiches; restaurant meals in the evening 6pm–9.30pm. Children and muddy walkers welcome; prefer no dogs.

Oriel y Felin, Trefin. Proprietors: Angela Samuel and Pauline Beynon; tel: 01348 837500. This is an Art Gallery with a tea room serving light lunches and clotted cream teas, specialising in the use of quality local produce. Open 11am–5pm during the season; out of season, please telephone first. There is wheelchair access and disabled toilet facilities. Children and muddy walkers are welcome; dogs in the garden.

Artramont Arms, Croesgoch. Proprietor: Ray Nadollek; tel: 01348 831309. Lunch, evening meal and children's menu. Disabled access. Welcomes walkers and dogs in the bar.

The Ship Inn, Trefin. Proprietors: Muriel and Mike Petersen; tel: 01348 831445. Bar meals, coffee and sandwiches all day; lunch 12pm–2.30pm, evening meal 6.30pm–9.30pm. Children welcome; no dogs.

Trevaccoon, Llanrhian. Proprietor: Caroline Flynn; tel: 01348 831438. Country house bed and breakfast; en suite rooms and disabled facilities. No evening meals.

The Sloop Inn, Porthgain. Proprietors: Matthew Blakiston and Brian Goddard; tel: 01348 831449. Bar meals and 'Finer Choice' menu, lunch and evening meal; every day except Christmas Day. Breakfast and afternoon tea in summer months; tea and coffee all day. Children's licence; no dogs. Muddy walkers welcome.

Tafarn Sinc, Rosebush. Proprietors: Brian and Brenda Llewellyn; tel: 01437 532214. Tea, coffee and sandwiches all day, all year. Full lunch menu summer only, evening meal throughout summer but Wednesday, Thursday, Friday and Saturday only in winter. Children's menu available. Muddy walkers welcome; no dogs. Built of corrugated iron sheeting, Tafarn Sinc stands on the platform of the north Pembrokeshire railway below the Rosebush slate quarries. It was quite a tourist attraction at the end of the 19th century and the present owners have recreated the atmosphere of the times, down to the sawdust on the bar floor.

The Old Post Office, Rosebush. Proprietor: Ruth Jones; tel: 01437 532205. Open from 11am. Lunches, tea, coffee, sandwiches, snacks, home-made cakes and evening meals from 7pm. Caters for vegetarian and vegan diets and welcomes children. Muddy walkers welcome but no dogs in the restaurant.

Drover's Arms, Puncheston. Proprietors: Martin and Jaynee Percival; tel: 01348 881469. Lunches (except Monday) 12pm–2.30pm; evening meals 6pm–9pm. Tea, coffee, sandwiches and filled baguettes available all day. Children and muddy walkers welcome; no dogs.

Dyffryn Arms, Pontfaen, Gwaun valley. Proprietor: Bessie Davies. Beer, soft drinks, crisps and company. No food but an experience. Local wisdom claims that anyone who sits in Bessie's for a year will emerge speaking Pembrokeshire Welsh like a native.

The Bush Inn, Robeston Wathen. Manager: David Crocker; tel: 01834 860778. Bar meals, à-la-carte menu and children's menu for lunch, 11am–2.30pm; evening meals 6pm–8.30pm. Muddy boots and well-behaved dogs allowed in bar and in a large play area outside.

The Pump on the Green, Spittal. Proprietor: Ricky McIntyre; tel: 01437 741339. Bar meals available 12pm–7pm. Booking ahead may be advisable for the restaurant. Children and muddy walkers welcome, though shoes may need to be removed if using the restaurant. Dogs are welcome in the bar.

The Wolfe Inn, Wolf's Castle. Proprietor: Giani di Lorenzo; tel: 01437 741676. Bar meals and à-la-carte menu, morning coffee, lunch 12pm–2pm, dinner 6pm–9pm. Recommended in the *Welsh Tourist Guide* and *Good Food Guide*. En suite accommodation available. Children welcome and well-behaved dogs allowed in the restaurant.

Cross Inn, Hayscastle Cross. Proprietors: Mr and Mrs Girlach; tel: 01348 840216. Traditional home-cooked lunches and evening meals with full children's menu, sandwiches and tea and coffee. Dogs allowed in the bar on the lead and muddy walkers welcome.

Victoria Inn, Roch. Proprietor: Julie Roberts; tel: 01437 710426. Bar meals, lunches, early evening meal (children's menu available) and tea and coffee all day. Muddy walkers welcome and dogs allowed in the bar.

Further Reading

B. G. Charles, *The Place-Names of Pembrokeshire* (Aberystwyth: The National Library of Wales, 1992)

J. Wyn Evans, *St Davids Cathedral* (Pitkin Guides; Andover: Jarrold Publishing, 2002)

Richard Fenton, *A Historical Tour through Pembrokeshire* (1811). A facsimile of the 1903 edition was published by the Cultural Services department of Dyfed County Council in 1994.

Francis Jones, *Historic Pembrokeshire Homes and their Families*, ed. Caroline Charles Jones (extended edition; Dinas: Brawdy Books, 2001)

Francis Jones, *The Holy Wells of Wales* (Cardiff: University of Wales Press, 1954, 1992)

W. B. Jones and E. A. Freeman, *The History and Antiquities of St Davids* (1856). Reprinted by the Cultural Services department of Dyfed County Council in 1998.

George Owen, *A Description of Penbrokshire* (1603). There is a modern edition with a life and preface by Dillwyn Miles (The Welsh Classics series; Llandysul: Gomer Press, 1994)

Nona Rees, *St David of Dewisland* (Llandysul: Gomer Press, 1992)

Nona Rees and Terry John, *Pilgrimage: A Welsh Perspective* (Llandysul: Gomer Press, 2002)

Siân Rees, *A Guide to Ancient and Historic Wales: Dyfed* (CADW Guide; London: HMSO, 1992)

Rhygyfarch, *Rhygyfarch's Life of St David*, tr. J. W. James (Cardiff: University of Wales Press, 1967)

Edward Yardley, *Menevia Sacra*, ed. Francis Green (printed for the Cambrian Archaeological Association; London: Bedford Press, 1927)